A Window on the Sea

Also by Daniel Farson

JACK THE RIPPER

MARIE LLOYD AND MUSIC HALL

OUT OF STEP

THE MAN WHO WROTE DRACULA

IN PRAISE OF DOGS

DANIEL FARSON

A Window on the Sea

ILLUSTRATED BY
John Dyke
OF BOSCASTLE

The Quality Book Club
London 1979

The Quality Book Club
125 Charing Cross Road
London WC2H 0EB

This edition by arrangement with
Michael Joseph Ltd.

Printed and bound in Great Britain by
REDWOOD BURN LIMITED
Trowbridge & Esher

For Frances with my love.

ACKNOWLEDGEMENTS

I should like to express my gratitude to the following: Nigel Buxton, for allowing me to quote from his travel column in the *Sunday Telegraph*, and John Anstey, for allowing me to use material published in *The Daily Telegraph Magazine*.

Ken Thomson, for giving me permission to reproduce extracts from my book *In Praise of Dogs*, George G. Harrap & Co., Ltd., 1976. Lillian Thomson, for her encouragement, and permission to quote from *Ilfracombe's Yesterdays*. And for the invaluable information contained in the following booklets: *The History of Georgeham and Croyde* by H. Stevenson Balfour, *Victorian Days in a Devon Village* by A. H. Slee, *Appledore—Handmaid of the Sea* by John Beara, *Two Villages* by R. F. Bidgood. To my friend, Dennis Knight, for his advice and permission to quote from 'Lundy's little airline' (*Aeroplane Monthly*, December 1975).

Many books have proved helpful in my research. In particular I am indebted to *Charles Kingley's Landscape* by Susan Chitty, David & Charles, 1976. I should also like to recommend: *Lundy—Tempestuous Isle* by Colonel Etherton and Vernon Barlow, Lutterworth Press, 1950; *Lundy Isle of Puffins* by Richard Perry, Lindsay Drummond, 1940; and *Home in Ham* by R. W. Thompson, Arrowsmith, providing a useful and charming account of Georgeham before the war, for which I am grateful. Above all I should like to thank Henry Williamson for his generous consent in letting me quote extensively from the books of his which have recorded this part of the world so finely: *Life in a Devon Village*, Faber & Faber; *Tales of a Devon Village*, Faber & Faber; *As the Sun Shines* (containing extracts from *The Dream of Fair Women*, 1924, and *Tarka the Otter*, 1927), Faber & Faber.

The books on the Blasket Islands have been reissued by Oxford University Press: *An Old Woman's Reflections* by Peig Sayers; *The Islandman* by Tomas O. Crohan; *Twenty Years a-Growing* by Maurice O'Sullivan.

A wind's in the heart of me, a fire's in my heels,
I am tired of brick and stones and rumbling waggon-wheels;
I hunger for the sea's edge, the limits of the land,
Where the wild old Atlantic is shouting on the sands.

John Masefield, *A Wanderer's Song*

chapter one

Back to earth

Sometimes a moment from the past comes winging back and I shiver with thoughts of might-have-been. Then I look through my window on to the sands below, with the grey, thunderous Atlantic beyond and Lundy Island dim in the distance. The treacherous self-pity subsides. I know I made the right decision.

At the time, in 1964, when I chucked a top job in television, my friends thought I was mad or had been given the sack. They could not comprehend that anyone would choose to exchange the glitter of TV fame for the slog of a self-employed writer. As far as security was concerned, they were right. But it was partly the exaggerated importance attached to television that made me quit.

I was beginning to realise that television was a substitute for life. A recent survey states that 92 per cent of us list 'watching television' as our favourite 'leisure activity'. *Activity?* It is the passivity of television that is ultimately so deadening, turning us into observers of life rather than participants in it. We watch more and more and do less and less. One original picture seen in an art gallery, or, better still, painted by yourself, is worth a hundred reproductions shown on the box; anyone who reads a book is involved because he contributes; even a visit to the cinema is an occasion: you go out, probably queue up, sit down and look upwards at the screen—you retain your objectivity, whereas you slouch before your TV set like a twentieth-century zombie.

The glamour of being labelled a 'TV Personality' becomes a mockery. Viewers idealise an image, not a real person. *Anyone* who appears on television often enough, doing *anything*, can win such easy popularity. No wonder Gilbert Harding called us 'telephoneys'. When I opened a fête, or made a speech, or crowned a beauty queen—all of which I did abominably—I felt I was a fraud. Recently, an advertisement for a gardening firm in Cheshire invited people to its showrooms to see a 'cardboard cut-out of Percy Thrower'. In 1964 I was in danger of becoming a cardboard cut-out myself.

Above all, I wanted to find out if I could write. I have had ten books published in the last five years and am still unsure of the answer: all I know is that I gain more satisfaction from the achievement of the written word. It was not the easy way out, but it was a necessity to place my life in the balance. Nor was it 'opting out'. Far from getting away from it all, my departure from London meant getting back to everything that mattered.

I enjoyed my career in television, especially the early days of exploration; the fun I had while managing The Waterman's Arms on the Isle of Dogs; the home I made on the bend of the river at Limehouse. I have always felt this need to live close to the water and I spent months searching for such a house in London. I found it at last above a barge repair yard along one of the busiest parts of the Thames. At high tide it was possible to dive off the balcony, if anyone was mad enough to risk the murk and floating timber. It was unspoilt then, fashionable now, with the row of derelict houses stretching to The Bunch of

Grapes, a trendy pub occupied by paperback publisher, painter, TV personality and Foreign Secretary.

But I wanted to get back to earth, to the rough, grey stone house waiting for me on the shores of North Devon, left to me by my parents. Mad perhaps to abandon success, but madder still to have such a place and stay there for two weeks in the year like a visitor on holiday. Or so I thought.

Today I am certain that if I had lingered in London my life would be the poorer. Do I protest too much? Let me explain.

The luxuries of living here are undramatic. My most memorable day of the year came in May, when nothing spectacular happened. I had been wanting to visit the graveyard at Morte Point on the other side of the bay—I can just distinguish the outline from my balcony.

My two constant companions here are my goddaughter Frances, and Peter Bradshaw; they look after the house, the garden and the dogs. I am indebted to them more than I can express in words, for they are not the people to enjoy seeing their names in print. But the contentment of life at the Grey House in recent years is largely due to them. When I have to leave, it is good to know they are looking after the house and the animals. On this occasion they were on holiday, so I set out alone with the dogs—which meant I was not really alone at all.

It was cloudy at first, but brightened up as we walked along the shore. I had meant my walk to coincide with the lowest moment of the tide, but in fact I had to scramble over the rocks at Woolacombe, perform a tightrope act along an iron pipe, jump over pools and even wade through water—the dogs swimming behind me. They were unamused until we reached the shelter of Barricane Beach and climbed up the cliffs to a bench where I dried off and rested. The dogs raced around the brambles in search of rabbits, while I ate a couple of hard-boiled eggs.

I can see Morte Point every day in the year, but I had forgotten the subtle serenity of the lie of the land, the quantities of wild sea pinks and the brightness of the gorse. As I sat there, looking across to Vention at the other end of the bay—a scattering of seven houses, my own discernible by the shining reflection on the grey slate roof—I experienced a sudden sense of exhilaration, almost of ecstasy. We walked back later that afternoon, tired and deeply satisfied, under a sky that was cloudless in the perfect warmth of a spring sun.

Can there be days when there is magic in the air? I dismissed such an elfin thought hastily, ashamed of such whimsy. Yet the following Sunday I read Nigel Buxton's travel feature in the *Sunday Telegraph*, of a walk he made along the cliffs further down the coast near Port Quin:

> . . . though I might call up every aid in *Roget's Thesaurus*, I know, sadly, that no written account of mine can do it justice; the full joy of it must live and die in what passes for my soul.
>
> Lovely? I have travelled on every continent, sailed on every ocean, seen all but a few of the world's acknowledged wonders (a credential; not a boast) and I swear I have never seen greater beauty, rarely known greater exaltation, seldom felt deeper joy than the beauty and the exaltation and the joy I felt and knew on the 14th of May, on that English shore.

I checked with my diary. The 14th of May—it was the same day. Was it a coincidence that we had shared a particularly glorious moment of spring? Or was it something more, to have made us feel so deeply? I do not know. But I too have gone round the world and seen many of its wonders, and I too have never seen greater beauty than I did on that 14th of May.

That night I felt absolute peace of mind. And *that* is one of the priceless luxuries of living here.

The old year ends in murder

Seldom have I enjoyed a New Year's Eve more. Never have I celebrated less. At the stroke of midnight I turned off the television set, toasted Bonzo, who lay at the foot of the bed, with a small glass of peach brandy—a residue from Christmas—turned off the light and fell instantly into a deep sleep.

The season of forced gaiety was over at last. Perhaps Christmas was a *day* once upon a time; now it seems to go on for weeks with nothing and nobody working, an everlasting Sunday with Bing Crosby on the radio singing interminably about Christmas as if he knew no other season; spangled frumps with whips subduing tigers on television; or mincing middle-aged negroes in pink suits, swaying as they chant about 'lurve' with their hands clasped in prayer and gigantic Christmas balls behind them.

I was thankful it was over.

Only one incident marred the tranquillity of the evening.

Returning before Christmas Eve, Frances and Peter had been racing down the motorway when they noticed a scrap of yellow fly out of the container-van in front of them. It was a chick, bound for some battery farm, miraculously torn free. Cars screamed over it. Frances protested weakly, but they stopped the Triumph and Peter dived into the motorway traffic, reappearing with the tiny creature. She became known as Ermintrude.

Having escaped death by inches, she spent the rest of the journey wrapped cosily in a scarf in the glove compartment. When I saw her first she looked like a child's fluffy toy, as if she had just been shampooed. I did not rate her chances of survival highly, but my pessimism was disregarded: 'Wait till she lays her first brown egg and I eat it in front of you with hot buttered toast!' It never occurred to us that Ermintrude might have been a cockerel.

Confounding my predictions, she grew rapidly. At first she was kept in a cardboard box in a hot cupboard open to the light, fed with Ready Brek. Her down was gradually replaced by small white wings. A few days later she was able to peck about on the grass when she was taken outside. Her chirping was surprisingly strong for such a tiny animal, and continuous except when she was stroked. If Peter called her, she came running as if she recognised her saviour.

Plainly, Ermintrude was a survivor—against the odds. More than that, an inspiration, for we started to think in earnest of keeping hens, not just as company for Ermintrude, more for the pleasure of fresh eggs for ourselves. Peter started to clear some land above the house to make a run, but on New Year's Eve he stayed in bed, with flu. While Frances drove to Braunton for medicine, I took the dogs for a long, wet walk along the sand-dunes. After they were fed, they joined me in my bedroom while I tried to concentrate on my writing.

Crunch—crunch—crunch! Bassey was in her favourite corner cupboard, thumping her tail on the floor as she contentedly munched a bone. *What bone?* They had been fed with tins of dog food.

I turned to see the last of Ermintrude's yellow legs disappearing into Bassey's mouth—I thought that 'crunch' had sounded different. With the sheepish look of a black-and-white sheepdog, which she claims to be, Bassey licked her lips and thumped her tail harder. All that was left of Ermintrude was a small pile of entrails.

Vainly, I hoped it was an illusion; it took a few moments for the horror to be confirmed as I hurried down the passage to find the door of the room open. Someone had forgotten to close it— me. No longer confined to the hot cupboard, Ermintrude's new home had been a box with a piece of chicken wire resting loosely on top. She might have escaped from this herself; either way she was easy prey for the predatory Bassey, now thrown out of doors with a sharp smack. As Bassey is pure animal and had only obeyed her instinct, she was soon forgiven.

Most of the hens I have known are irritating animals, unlike ducks, which retain their charm. But Ermintrude was special and would have continued to give happiness even if she had never laid an egg. Glimpses of those yellow feet returned to haunt me in the evening.

She has proved the importance of having other animals around the place, apart from the dogs. A goat, perhaps? Certainly, we are determined to keep chickens.

The new year has opened with the sound of hammering outside, as Peter starts to build a henhouse from driftwood.

The solace of winter

The view from my window is never the same. I look out on to Baggy Point as I write, and find it is different yet again: red-brown today and sombre, while the sea is hard to describe—more than grey and certainly less than blue.

I wake in the morning and know that when I draw the curtains I shall be surprised. When I mentioned this to a friend, he pointed out that *every* place changes all the time, only we fail to notice it. Perhaps this is true, but it is impossible not to notice the changes here: the gradual progress of the sunsets moving behind

Baggy Point until one evening when the sun appears beyond the land and sinks into the sea, and I know that spring is here. The turn of the tides that can surge right up to the wooden steps, and then go out again for half a mile. A scarlet sunset signifying bad weather.

Not only does the view look different; it sounds different. Sometimes I wake up and feel there is something unusual; then I realise what it is—the silence. Most of the time, the sea maintains an uproar that I take for granted until there is a sudden calm. Two nights ago there was such a battering wind that the electricity failed so I had to read by candlelight and cook on my open fire: I was disappointed when the lights flashed on again. Today there is the stillness after a storm, and I am conscious of the lack of noise.

When I moved down here, I thought I might stay in the summer months and return to London for the bright lights of a city in winter. The opposite has happened. I welcome the storms and wood fires more than the crowded months of July and August. Anyhow, our weather seems to be changing: the winters are milder, followed swiftly by the radiance of April and May. Then there is the golden afterglow of October. These are the best months.

I am aware of the seasons as never before. January is supposed to be a dormant month, but I have noticed the first daffodils, a few of them in bud already, and have picked the first camellias, which look so delicate with their pink lines traced on cream—though they must be incredibly tough.

Baggy Point lining the southern side of the bay; Morte Point on the north. While Baggy is bold and fierce, the folds of the cliffs charging into the sea, Morte seems softer. The gentleness is deceptive and the name is no accident: 'Mortehoe' meaning 'point of death' and Morte Stone, stuck in the sea a hundred yards beyond, notoriously dangerous to passing ships. These were not helped, according to legend, by the local habit of tying lanterns on to the tails of cows to lure the unsuspecting captains into an apparent harbour with the lights of ships swinging at anchor. According to Henry Williamson, the sands are haunted by a sea captain who was the only survivor of such a wreck.

When a farmer's wife discovered him as he was washed ashore, and saw his lips trying to speak, she held his head under the water with the prongs of a pitchfork until he was drowned. Any furniture from the ship that had not been smashed to pieces on the rocks ended in the farmhouse, where it was noticed by the captain's wife who had travelled from Scotland to claim his body. An argument ended in a curse. Subsequently, the farmer died unexpectedly, his wife went mad, and now when a south-west gale is blowing, the headless ghost of 'Cap'n Harry' rides a white horse across the sands.

Below Mortehoe lies Barricane Beach—covered with shells and fragments of shells—and further back, in the corner of the bay, lies the holiday village of Woolacombe. Place names fascinate me. In this case the village is supposed to be named after a family called 'Woolacombe'. There are several families in North Devon with the prefix of 'Wool', such as Woolacott and Woolaway, but 'combe' implies valley; hence Combe Martin, and Ilfracombe named after King Alfred—Alfredescumbe. One authority even suggests that Woolacombe is derived from Wulfa Combe—a valley of wolves. My favourite derivation is that of Wiveliscombe, a town not far from Taunton. Apparently there was a mining centre here and workers were brought from the north without their families. Consequently, it became known as 'the wifeless valley'—'wifeless combe'. Further north, the name of Bridgwater would seem self-explanatory, yet is named after the first Norman owner, *Walter* de Douai.

The cluster of houses where I live, at the other end of Woolacombe Bay, is known as Vention. It is an attractive name, used by my parents on their letterhead and still found on maps, though few people use it today. Vention Sands are better known as Putsborough Sands, after the low thatched manor house and farm buildings that lie a mile beyond the skyline. In the 1920s Henry Williamson described a walk when Vention Lane was sunken under banks and little more than the width of a horse-butt. He referred to the two perfectly simple, side-by-side cottages, the only houses in this corner of 'the loveliest bay in the West Country' up to the First World War, and claimed they were known as the Cottages of the New Invention 'since they had been built with chimneys, which were, apparently, the new invention'. That is one explanation of the name. The present owner, the Earl of Dudley, has another which seems more convincing: that the chimney referred to was the adjacent limekiln, and *that* was the new invention. This is confirmed by a reference in Risdon's *Survey of Devon* (1630): 'Of late a new invention has sprung up and has been practised, by burning lime and incorporating it with earth for a season and then spread upon the arable land, and hath produced a plentiful increase of all sorts of grain amongst us, where formerly it never grew in any man's memory'.

Several limekilns were built along the coast. Boats brought the limestone, which was heaved over the side and pulled up the shore by horses when the tide went out. The lime was also used for whitewash.

Originally, the two simple cottages in the corner were the homes of the lime-burners, then they were used by coastguards, and finally converted into the single residence known as Vention Cottage. There have been further additions made by Lord Dudley, such as a splendid sea-wall built with rare craftsmanship, and the kiln remains. Its attractive shape, with the arch below, proves that some man-made objects can enhance the landscape.

Why we settled here

My parents stayed in a guest-house at Woolacombe in the last war, when my father was asked to write a film script called *Blitz Hotel* for the actor Clive Brook. It would have made an excellent film, but the producer shot himself. At least my parents had found the bay and noted the few houses at Vention. They returned to rent a comfortable bungalow called Sedgebanks, which I visited in my teens, and my father completes the story in his book *A Mirror for Narcissus:*

> . . . a house we had often wished we owned as we saw it when walking along the sands—a little grey house, built of the local stone, standing on its own isolated plateau overlooking the sea—came into the market. Its owner, appropriately enough, had died in Kenya [a country my father knew well]. This house was the only land on his estate that was not entailed.

His son wanted some ready money to pay the death duties, so we made him a price and he took it. We thought it was the most sensible thing we had ever done in our life. And just about in time.

When I moved here after their deaths, I felt the same way. My father was outraged to find no evidence that the previous occupants had read a book. While my mother painted the walls to hide a dreadful shade of chocolate, my father set up a work-bench in the garage and built bookshelves with planks of Oregon pine that had been washed ashore after a storm. Today the house is lined with books and it has been a source of satisfaction to add my few publications to the long line of my father's—*The Way of a Transgressor* in numerous editions and translations—along the top shelf of the bookcase in our living-room.

He wrote about this house, with considerable pride and pleasure, in 1956:

Only the roof of our house shows from the little private road that leads past these six homes. We are the only people who live here all the year round, except another writer and his wife who are just as farouche as we are: we sometimes don't speak to one another for a month. This lonely part of the coast has, thank God, no drop-inners: we can be as isolated as if marooned on a desert island. We have left the slope and plateau before our house, overlooking the sea, just as nature made it. The fine turf that grows on these windswept downs has an amazing number of gay wild flowers that come in their seasons; there are masses of sea campion, and primroses in spring on all the grassy banks. We have even left the ferns in their natural state along the edge of our plateau. I think their delicate tracery is one of the most beautiful designs in all nature, but they can be a damned nuisance when they start to march across your place. From the end of September to nearly the end of May no footmarks mar these three miles of sand, except those of the coastguard on his dawn patrol, or of a few gatherers of driftwood. Sitting in my bed at dawn, or on sleepless moonlit nights, I look straight out on the Atlantic Ocean. I might as well be in a ship at sea. This makes one broody. Self-searching is part of the mood of this place; the sound of the sea is all about you, though after a time you cease to be conscious of it.

Twenty years later there is still this degree of solitude in winter, and of course that is one of the blessings of being here. There are days when I see no one else on the sands, or just a solitary silhouette in the distance—and even that seems an intruder. As for the self-searching, I echo those moods too—which is no bad thing.

I sympathise with my father's insomniac melancholy. As a foreign correspondent he had covered the world, but it is a fallacy to think that wanderlust can be assuaged. It grows more compelling. At times his resolve broke down and London became irresistible. Though it was no longer the city he had loved in his heyday, he set off with such high hopes of company and conversation.

> The danger, of course, was that I went in over my head every time I stepped out of this mood. The train to London meant the luxury of sitting in the dining-car, of watching the clouds pass by over the rolling West Country, and of gin after gin after gin . . .
>
> I won't say that I regret those gin-inspired reveries, but by the time the train reached Waterloo I had already lost the game.

Again, and all too often, I have followed in those footsteps. The sudden contrasts between solitude and a surfeit of food and drink and conversation, between the breezes off the Atlantic and the oven-airlessness of hotels, are hard to reconcile.

My father retained his wanderlust—he was tying labels on his luggage a few seconds before he collapsed and died—but he never failed to appreciate what he found here.

> Sometimes, sitting up on the downs and watching the ships headed in for the Bristol Channel; or worse, watching some ship going *out*—the smoke from her freshly-stoked fires trailing behind her like a black rope—I have felt a madness of frustration. [But] . . . when I thought things over carefully, I knew that I was lucky in my coastal paradise here in North Devon. I think it is one of the most noble stretches of sea and sand anywhere in the world.

He had discovered, before it was too late, the value of compromise—a word that I detested when young as something to be avoided at all costs. And what a lot of unnecessary anguish that caused me.

I interviewed my father three times on television. On the last occasion, shortly before his death on 13 December 1960, he pointed out to Baggy Point and exclaimed: 'This is the perfect place for journey's end.'

Rescued from Baggy

My journey almost came to an end when I was twenty and tried to swim round Baggy Point. My parents were renting Sedgebanks at the time, and I was on a fortnight's leave from the American army—for I had dual nationality then—with a fellow GI from Germany called Henry Compton. He was a sergeant; I had just been promoted to corporal.

It was the first week of September, with a last glare of summer. To start with, the expedition was easy as we scrambled over the rocks or swam round them. I was unaware of the names then, but we passed Ramsom Cliff and Bloodhill Cliff where the Norsemen were supposed to have fought the English. The Norse chieftains, Crida and Putta, allegedly gave their names to the villages of Croyde and Putsborough further inland. Earlier still, the Vikings had occupied Baggy and the quantity of flints and arrow-heads ploughed up around Baggy Farm suggests that their settlement was extensive. A wild place to have chosen unless the very exposure made it safer from attack, with little chance of surprising it from the sea.

The cliffs at the end are tremendous and sheer, and the cave known as Baggy Hole goes so far back that when a dog was taken inside and ran away, it was 'next seen in Barnstaple'. At least this is the unlikely story told by John Page in his guidebook *Coasts of Devon*, published in 1895. I wish I had read his book before setting out that afternoon in September, for he gave fair warning:

> Except in very calm weather, with the wind from the east or
> south, the attempt cannot be made, and even then there is

some risk, owing to the sudden, and very often unaccountable, rising of a ground sea. To get at the place over the cliffs is almost impossible, though I know one man who has done it with safety at low water of spring tides. But he had no time for more than a short visit before the tide turned, and he had to decamp hurriedly. Another daring visitor was caught, and spent four dreadful hours climbing the cliffs, cutting notches in the shale with his pocket knife.

We had no knives—our swimming trunks were our only protection, though we were armour-plated by our foolish optimism. The idea of entering Baggy Hole from the sea, with the hope of seeing the grey seals basking at the entrance, seemed like a mild adventure when the sea was calm. But the sea can turn in the instant. The jagged rocks may look more harmful, but it is the water that demands a constant respect. When the tide flows, the current is so strong that it is impossible to row against—the best procedure is to drift out and start again when the tide slackens. Of course you only realise the treachery of the water when you are on it. To add to the deception, small coasters pass unnervingly close—a few feet away from the rocks—with the easy strength of their engines. The water here is deep, and if the captains skirted further out—where it *looks* safe—they would be in danger of striking the isolated rock that rises from the surf on certain days with an explosion of spray, like a polaris missile.

Just around the point, another rock caused the shipwreck of HMS *Weazle* on 11 February 1799 and has been known as Weazle's Rock ever since. All the crew were lost—105 men—and some are buried in the churchyard at Georgeham. A verse recorded the tragedy of the wreck:

> Who hath escaped
> From the tempest's fell sweep
> From the crunch of her timbers,
> On Baggy's dark leap?
> Not a soul! There was one
> Left behind on the shore,
> His fortune to thank
> But his friends to deplore.

Unaware of these alarming precedents, we continued round

the point. The day was so still that the possibility of a sudden sea-change did not occur to us, but as we rounded the point the swell rose with a vengeance. It surged up the rocks for ten or fifteen feet and fell violently back. We watched without too much dismay at first, naïve enough to imagine that it might die down. The cliffs defied contemplation. I am surprised expert mountaineers haven't used them as a practice climb, unless even they—with all their ropes and tackle—regard the sheer drop as too hazardous.

Today, I have convinced myself that I was prepared to swim further on to the next rock, with the hope of being lifted by the now gigantic swell and dropped near the one tortuous track that might have led us to the top. It might be the self-flattery of time that makes me believe my companion surveyed the increasing turbulence and decided against it. Either way, I remember I was relieved.

In quick succession, the air grew colder, the swell became more ferocious, and the sun disappeared over the horizon. The darkness fell as if we were in the Mediterranean. Almost before we were aware of what had happened, we were shivering on a rock with the sea advancing every moment. We could tell that by the noise. Time became meaningless, but it must have been several hours before we noticed a faint light on the cliffs above us. Then more lights, and distant shouts that were unintelligible in the wind. Unknown to us, policemen, doctors, two fire-engines with rockets and the coastguard service had come to our rescue—alerted by my father, who knew my appetite and realised something was wrong when I failed to return for dinner.

They were more alarmed than we were, for they knew that the high-water mark of the tide was above the rock on which we were perched. Coastguards tried to descend with ropes but the fifty-foot drop was too complicated. Then the rockets were fired, landing their lifelines within reach of us. I hate to imagine what we should have done then, but at this moment the Clovelly lifeboat plunged through the waves playing its searchlight over the rocks until it found us. By now, the swell was so powerful that the coxswain, George Lamey, was forced to anchor thirty feet out to avoid being smashed on the rocks while a dinghy was rowed towards us by two volunteers. As I jumped, I fell into the sea, but was pulled on board and within a few minutes we were safely on the lifeboat, wrapped in blankets, fortified with rum and biscuits. A newspaper reported dramatically: 'As the dinghy returned to the lifeboat waves began to break over the top of the rock, and it was quickly submerged by the tide.'

When we reached Clovelly we were treated for exposure and stayed the night at the Red Lion Hotel on the quayside. Curiously, I had not felt in the slightest danger throughout—death by drowning has always struck me as a better fate than most. The real victim was my father, who felt so mortified by the whole incident that he donated a handsome silver trophy to future lifeboat crews unfortunate enough to be called out at midnight to rescue fools from rocks.

chapter two

Clovelly fisherman

Clovelly does not change much over the years, if you go there out of season as I have just done. It remains the same because change has been made so difficult. It is a village where no cars drive up and down because they are unable to, and where the cottages with their small gardens of flowers and shrubs remain unconverted because they are rented and the regulations are strict.

None of this is accidental. Clovelly remains unspoilt because it is one of the last villages in England owned by a private estate. Hardly a window-box can be added without permission. Such control creates a mixture of pride and resentment among the villagers, but if the owners make a small fortune from the summer visitors they should also receive the credit for keeping Clovelly intact.

The usual excrescences of gifte-shoppes and car parks with

toilets are kept out of sight above the village. An incredible half-million tourists descend the steep cobbled street in summer, but when they have left the village comes into its own again. And if you go there in November, when the surrounding red-brown woods have the wistfulness of a Victorian engraving, or on a bleak but honest day in January, you will find the village as tranquil as it used to be.

There is disagreement over the name Clovelly. Some say it comes from the Latin *clausa vallis*—a closed glen—or *cloh* meaning ravine. As *cleave* was the Saxon for cliff, I should have thought that cleave-valley was another possible derivation. Equally, it might be a corruption of *cleave-leigh*, the cliff place, as the manor was called in the Domesday Book.

The most famous owners of Clovelly were the Giffards in the eleventh century; the Carys from the fourteenth to the eighteenth centuries; and finally the Hamlyns. The entire estate was bought in 1738 by Zachary Hamlyn for £9,426, which seems a pittance now but was a considerable sum then. Mrs Christine Hamlyn is remembered still and her initials can be seen on the cottages she renovated. She referred imperiously to her parishioners as 'my people' and she died in 1936. At her memorial service the Archbishop of Canterbury thanked God 'for her strong, stimulating and radiant personality, for the warmth and generosity of her friendship, for the charm, the incisiveness, the humour of her conversation, for her ever vigilant protection of the beauty of her beloved Clovelly, for the mingled masterfulness and tenderness of her rule . . .' Even allowing for the flattery of bishops, she sounds exceptional.

The owners had complete autonomy. They had the right to take the law into their own hands, even to the hanging of their prisoners. Their power was absolute partly because Clovelly was as isolated as an island, easier to reach by sea than by land. Even today, as you fly along the coastline down to Hartland Point, the landscape below seems surprisingly virgin, with the solitary farm and the white cascade of Clovelly houses halfway along.

Of the early legends about the village, the most colourful concerns the family of John Gregg—eight sons, six daughters and countless grandchildren—who inhabited a cave near Mouth Mill and made a living by robbing lonely travellers. Their food came from the same source: the limbs of the people they murdered and pickled, for the Greggs were cannibals. They practised cannibalism for twenty-five years until one of their victims managed to escape and give the alarm. Rumours had been spreading with the disappearance of so many people, and now troops and dogs searched the area where the man had been attacked. When they reached the entrance to the cave, the dogs began to howl. The Greggs were burnt to death, all forty-six of them. It is an unexpected story, recorded in several documents, and it is a shame to point out the comparison to the better-known Scottish cannibal, Sawney Bean, and his family. Probably the Greggs were part of a common folklore, based on fact.

Three physical features make Clovelly spectacular.

There is the cobbled street, down the middle of which ran a stream, with houses either side that somersault towards the sea. Sleds are used to carry provisions throughout the year, while the donkeys are brought out in the summer largely for the benefit of visitors, though they brought the post until a few years back.

Then there is the richness of the surrounding woods, of birch and oak, described by Charles Kingsley as a 'forest wall, five hundred feet high, of almost semi-tropical luxuriance'. Kingsley's father was the rector here, and Charles used many of the local names for his famous romance *Westward Ho!*, which gave its name to the resort a few miles further north—rather than the other way around, as most people imagine. Leaving Clovelly at the age of seventeen, Kingsley returned when he was thirty: 'I cannot believe my eyes,' he wrote to his wife, 'the same place, the same pavement, the same dear old smells, the dear old handsome loving faces again.' *Dear old smells*—the phrase grates curiously today, but smells are not what they used to be. What could be more redolent than the smell of tar, or new rope, or smoke from the limekiln that used to be fired below?

Charles Dickens, too, was captivated by the woodland. He used Clovelly as the setting for his short story *A Message from the Sea*, and made his sea captain slap his leg and exclaim in pleasure, 'A mighty sing'lar and pretty place it is, as ever I saw in all the days of my life.' Dickens described it in autumn:

The red-brown cliffs, richly wooded to their extremest verge, had their softened and beautiful forms reflected in the bluest water, under the clear North Devonshire sky of a November day without a cloud. The village itself was so steeped in autumn foliage from the houses lying on the pier to the top-most ladder that one might have fancied it was out a-bird's-nesting, and was, as indeed it was, a wonderful climber.

A three-mile road guides you through the surrounding dense-ness, with sudden panoramic views of the coastline and Clovelly itself. It is known as Hobby Drive, because this was the personal hobby of Sir James Hamlyn Williams, who supervised the con-struction from 1811 until his death eighteen years later. When part of it subsided at the turn of the century, a new stretch was substituted and called the Sailor's Cut because so many fisher-men were involved in its building.

The other feature that strikes you instantly is the harbour and the jutting jetty, with bollards reputed to be Spanish cannon sal-vaged after the Armada. The houses leaning in a row over the pebbled beach have changed slightly in their usefulness over the years: the limekiln, which supplied the houses with their white-wash, is dormant; the old lifeboat station built in 1870 has been replaced by a modern lifeboat moored permanently outside the harbour in case of emergency. But the limekiln and the old life-boat slipway are still there, if retired.

After the hazards of Hartland Point, ships have always wel-comed the natural harbour as a refuge. The protection was con-solidated by the quay-wall built during the fourteenth century from the immense stones washed up on the shingle beach, though how the heaviest were hoisted into place remains a mystery.

It was so arduous to reach Clovelly by land that visitors usually travelled by sea, across the Bristol Channel. Steamers anchored outside and adventurous ladies lifted their skirts as far as discretion permitted as they stepped from the dinghys onto the shore. At that time Clovelly was both a beauty spot and a work-ing port, with the harbour so crammed with fishing boats that the village was called the Brixham of the north coast. Charles Dickens gives a feeling of the busy atmosphere:

Strings of pack horses and pack donkeys toiled slowly up the staves of the ladders bearing fish and coal and such other cargo as was unshipped at the pier from the dancing fleet of village boats and two or three coasting traders. The pier was musical with the wash of the sea and the creaking of the capstans and the windlasses, and the airy fluttering of little vanes and sails. The rough sea bleached boulders of which the pier was made, and the white boulders of the shore were brown with drying nets.

Fishermen wove their lobster pots in the slack season and joined the fleets when the fish came in. Local cod was alleged to be 'the best in the world' but the most plentiful catch was the famous Clovelly herring. Sometimes the nets were so full there was no time to remove the fish as they were hauled on board, and they had to be towed into harbour with the fish still enmeshed, to be removed on shore later. Early photographs show lines of trawlers, revealing what a flourishing scene this used to be at the beginning of the last century, when herring were so abundant that on good days you could buy two or three hundred for a shilling.

And then, inexplicably, like the pilchard at Newquay, the Clovelly herring moved elsewhere. This undreamt-of disaster decimated the livelihood of the fishermen. A fine old photograph taken in 1903, entitled *Rest After Toil*, shows lines of them leaning up against a sea wall, smoking their pipes. They all wore hats, fine faces underneath and names that sound strong and old-fashioned too: Will Headon, Sam Shackson, Ganger Harris, 'Old Steve' Headon, Ambrose Pennington, Jamin Smale and Richard Headon. Today, there is only one full-time fisherman left in Clovelly—Si Headon, assisted by his son. Si, short for Josiah, was born on 3 December 1903, the same year that the photograph was taken to record his great-grandfather 'Old Steve' Headon, who lived to ninety-three. Si was born in a house on top of the hill, but soon his family moved to the quayside, to a house next to the lifeboat station. Many a visitor must have stared at it wistfully: 'The water lapped the walls,' says Si, 'and I've laid in bed times years ago, when I was a boy, and saw the rockets fired from the lifeboat slip up past my window.'

The sound of surf subsiding on stones—a surge and a slap and a sigh—is balm to me, but not to everyone. I quote from an old guidebook written by a traveller who stayed at the Red Lion: 'I have anything but joyful recollections of a night spent at a little inn on the quay of Clovelly. My room overlooked the sea, and all night long the waves and the pebbles between them kept up a perfect pandemonium. When I dropped asleep about three in the morning it was only to dream of express trains roaring past.'

'That would have been a visitor, would it,' Si replies, as if that explained everything. 'Had he been an inhabitant brought up on the seashore like I was, he wouldn't have taken any notice.' But even laconic Si remembers a tide that ran through their kitchen, and a great storm when a boulder—'nearly half a hundred-weight'—was lifted by the force of the sea and thrown on to the roof of the Red Lion Hotel. What would the guidebook writer have made of that?

Si's has been a lifetime devoted to the sea. He left school when he was fourteen to work as an apprentice to Blackmore's, the shipbuilders in Appledore. At first he was given a lift by the man who sold nets to the fishermen along the coast, arriving grandly in a horse-drawn cart. Later, he was able to afford a bicycle out of his wages—three shillings a week.

This was followed by a spell at Falmouth dockyards and then service with the British Oil Tanker Company as a carpenter until he returned to Clovelly, and stayed. Si has sailed round the world and remembers the fjords of Bergen with special pleasure, but he says that 'there is no country in the world like England and no place in the world like Clovelly'.

He is something of a cliché—a man who is happy in his work. It is not easy work either, no dangling of a line over the side. Helped by his son Norman, Si has to haul his boat across the pebbles and winch it gradually into the water—this is more arduous than the actual fishing. They go out regardless of rain or failing light and if Si was an ordinary man he would have retired years ago when he passed his seventieth birthday. As I discovered when I went out with them, the motive is not entirely greed, for the evening's catch can be trivial: mainly grey mullet with just a few of the famous herring, silver shapes meshed in the nets as Si pulls them on board.

'Were the Clovelly herring really so special?' I ask him.

'Exactly the same as any other herring,' he replies flatly, 'only the fish we catch are not mishandled or thrown into baskets as they are in most of the big ports. These are sold locally, fresh,

that is how they got their name.' He cooks them simply and
slowly in butter in a frying pan, keeping them basted. I bought a
few from that night's catch and cooked them the moment I
returned home. If it is true that a mackerel must be eaten soon
after it is caught, this must be even truer of herring. Now I
understand their fame—it was a new taste altogether.

Si speaks with satisfaction of the time he sank. He had caught
enough to make him pause, though less than his record catch of
nearly 10,000 fish.

'"Well Norman," I said, "I think we've got enough." I was
prepared to let the nets go, but he said, "I think we can manage
this one," and we did. We hauled the net in with the fish and at
that moment it was all right, but then the wind freshened from
the south-east. I saw what was going to happen and threw over as
many as three nets, but, do you know, the weather became so bad
we got overwhelmed and, of course, the boat sank.'

'Did you lose it?'

'Yes, I lost both the boat and the engine, but the people ashore
on the lookout, they discerned what was happening and the lifeboat was launched. Before the boat sank, I told Norman, I said,
"Norman my son, get your boots off, Norman, take your oil coat
off. Get everything off." He not being too well a swimmer. But
he kept calm, which I was very grateful about, and he kept afloat
with the help of the nets. I kept on saying to Norman, "All right
old boy, it's all right." At last I saw the lifeboat come round the
corner of the quay. I suppose we were only in the water half an
hour.'

When the lifeboat started to tow his boat, which was upside
down but afloat, the painter broke and it sank to the bottom.
They picked up the nets they had anchored and returned to
Clovelly with some of the fish, at least.

Today, Si has two boats and makes more from their 'trips
round the bay' in summer than he does from winter fishing. Si
has never fished on the Sabbath—'I was brought up that way'.

He points out to sea and remembers: 'I used to live out there.'
The longest time he was out was eighteen hours in his
rowboat—'We got so many herring in the net we couldn't haul
in and pick them out, and we couldn't get in the harbour because
the tide was out—so we drifted.' Darkness does not bother him,

nor the basking sharks that get entangled in his nets and drown. He has caught three, sixteen feet long, and 'knew' one that was twenty-five feet.

The decline in fishing, no longer an attractive occupation to the local boys, is one of his few disappointments: 'They trawl up tons of fish now, they're depleting the stocks, and with pollution on top of it I think the time is coming when fish will be scarce. It's not a good living round here any more and the youngsters won't do it. There ain't a lot of them stopping here now.'

When he was a boy, the families were bigger—he was one of nine children—and though thirty children lived along the quayside they came from only four families. A hundred and thirty-three went to the village school; now there are less than thirty. Hearing such recollections, Si seems to belong to a different age—and to a certain extent he does. He remembers when there were few strangers and no cars, only a horse-drawn carriage along the coast, and you had to get out and push as you went up the hills. Villagers went into Bideford on May Day, and possibly one other day a year. As for a visit to London, that was a fantasy—out of the question! He saw the last limestone for the kiln pulled ashore by donkeys in 1911, and remembers the stones on the beach taken away by barges to be used on roads that would finally bring the traffic. I suggest that in a further fifty years' time, the present village life may be a thing of the past. He disagrees—'I think they in Clovelly will carry on the same way as we always were; they will have their whist drives and their parties and the like; they will be a community unto itself.'

By today's more cynical standards, Si Headon might sound complacent. If he is, it is in the best sense—and why should dissatisfaction be preferable?

'Would you say you love the sea?' I ask him.

'Oh sure, it has really been completely my life. If ever a man has lived a full life, it's meself.'

'You seem a contented man.'

'Ah yes, I am contented in this manner—I don't think there is any man worked much harder than I have. That in itself makes you contented.'

When his wife tells him anxiously that she would rather have him home than out at sea, he replies, 'I feel fit enough and I'd rather wear out than rust out. I've known fellows give up—sit back in the chair—and they've gone! Oh yes, there is nobody could have a better life than I've had.'

Do I dare call him the salt of the earth? Anyhow, that is how I remember him, a roly-poly figure in his blue-knit Appledore jersey and a delightful shock of white hair as he takes off his cap to scratch his head. At that moment he has the look of a jovial donkey.

In January 1975, the villagers presented him with a parchment at the Parish Hall, the 'equivalent of the honorary freedom in the good old days when there were boroughs'. At one time he held a dozen honorary jobs in the parish simultaneously; for twenty years he was Secretary of the Missions to Seamen, and also the Church Warden. He has been the School Manager and Chairman of the Parish Council. Not surprising, then, that the newspaper described the event as 'Mr Clovelly to be honoured.'

Clovelly is more beautiful than picturesque; more genuine than the postcard image of donkeys up the cobbles. Planners—what a misnomer that is today!—should hasten to Clovelly and learn. Not one house is the same as another, yet there is a symmetry as they overlap and tumble down the cliff without a hint of discipline. The Hobby Drive was hailed in its day as 'a remarkable example of the new romantic appreciation of wild nature in her real wilderness, not trimmed to look wild, as it had still been the ideal of improvers a short time before'. In other words, not tamed as it would be now, with concrete bollards. It was a pleasure to see it from the water when I was out in the boat with Si. The waterfall on the northern side, known as Fresh Water; the prominence to the south known as Gallantry Bower.

Protected by the vigilance of the estate, and the enthusiasm of the local ladies who sweep in front of their cottages and pick up the litter of cigarette ends and matchsticks at six o'clock on summer mornings, there is every hope that Clovelly will remain the same.

Is it the prettiest village in Britain, as people claim? It had just been declared the winner of the Britain in Bloom Competition when I was there, but had not yet entered for the Prettiest Village. In one way, I hope they lose: 'pretty' is not the word for

Clovelly—it is rarer than that.

It's impossible to describe in a phrase: both Mediterranean and yet completely English. Go to Clovelly in the late autumn or early spring and you will understand.

chapter three

Of hens . . . and dogs

The chicken run is completed. Now for the chicks. We see them advertised in the *North Devon Journal* and phone to arrange to collect them. As they prove more expensive than I expected—£1.75 each—I decide on nine rather than ten.

The farm is on the edge of Exmoor on the way to Hunter's Inn, near the village of Trentishoe, and we go down a road with a 'No Vehicles' sign, past a field with a stream and horse, until we come to the farm.

A black Alsation puppy gives an initial bark, more friendly than ferocious, and runs off to chase one of several lurking cats. A couple of pigs, several indignant geese, a handsome white billy goat—and then the hens, about sixty of them, kept in a section of an outhouse. Nine are handed out and tied inside two large cardboard boxes we have brought with us. We are offered the handsome goat as well, but refuse, reluctantly.

Soon after we return home, a friend arrives, which seems lucky for he is a self-declared expert on most things and 'knows all about chickens'. After he has helped Frances to clip the wings, he comes in for tea and tells me how it's done: 'You cut through the *sides* of the feathers very carefully, without cutting their veins, so there is too much air going through to give them any pressure for lift-off . . .' I nod vaguely, my mind meandering, until I hear him say—'we balanced this carefully on both sides, so that . . .'

'*Oh no!*' I exclaim. Even I know that the whole point is to clip the wings on one side only, to unbalance the birds if they try to fly off. But there it is, and there they are, safe in the wooden hut that Peter has built in the run prepared above the house.

I wake to a raging gale. The sea is laced with white and the trees are thrashed by the wind, so it is hardly surprising that the hens take a beady look when I lower their drawbridge and refuse to set a claw outside. Hens are suspicious creatures anyhow, but these seem unusually cautious, flinching at a snatch of bird-song— and that only a sparrow's. We wonder if they have been 'hardened off' as the farmer assured us, for the great outdoors holds no appeal for them, even though they are twenty-two weeks old. Also, we have noticed something wrong with their beaks: either the upper beak has not developed, or the lower one sticks out too far. Consequently, they seem unable to pick up their grain. We leave them huddling woefully in their hut, their darting eyes registering total dismay their 'cheeps' resembling a faltering wireless SOS signal. But we return from a tempestuous walk to find that curiosity has proved stronger than the elements and all the chicks but one have ventured outside. Now for the prospect of fresh brown eggs.

My father said it would be a crime to live here without an animal. I had to overdo it and accumulate eight dogs. Such a number would be ludicrous in London—and it was. They were another reason for moving here, where they are absorbed. Even so, such a number was unintentional; it isn't fair to them. When they are puppies it is entertaining to see them all together, a stumbling procession, but as they grow older it is inevitable that some receive less attention than others—and it is an unpalatable fact that these are the duller. A one-man dog is stretched to his full personality.

I shall never know a dog to equal Littlewood, because I shall never be able to give so much to a dog again. Yet, from the first, she was extraordinary.

I have written before of her arrival when I was living in the East End of London at Limehouse, on the bend of the River Thames. It was a warm spring evening and I walked back from Cable Street, where I had been working on the film *Sparrows Can't Sing*, to find a small boy on my doorstep.

'Seen yer pup?' he asked.

'I don't have one.'

'You do now.'

I went upstairs to find a group of the local children, from the 'Buildings' opposite, prodding at something underneath the sofa. They pushed in saucers of milk and pieces of bread, but there was no reaction. Finally they pulled out a lifeless lump of black fur. Rose, my housekeeper, came in from the kitchen to explain that two of the boys had bought the puppy the day before in Petticoat Lane Market. The impulse to do so must have been irresistible, for they knew they were not allowed to keep animals in the 'Buildings' and this had been confirmed by their father who threatened to destroy the dog unless they found a new owner. The boys looked at the mongrel puppy, and then at me, without much hope.

'Heard you wanted a dog.'

'Yes, a guard dog to scare off burglars, a Doberman or an Alsation. Not *this*!' They watched me intently, like a pack of waiting wolves. 'Oh dear,' I thought, and asked aloud, 'What's she called?' There was a sigh of relief; they knew that they had won.

'Her name's Trix, Trixie, ain't it?'

'Oh no, it isn't!' I declared emphatically, trying to think of an appropriate name. I thought of Barbara Windsor and Joan Littlewood, with whom I had just been working. 'Barbara' seemed absurd for a dog, so did 'Joan' for that matter.

'I shall call her Littlewood,' I announced.

'That's not a dog's name,' said the boy scornfully.

'Because of the Pools,' explained Rose, mistakenly but prophetically.

This is how Littlewood became part of my life. When I

returned home later that night I was prepared to find her dead—
she was so young she could hardly feed herself. Instead, Littlewood emerged from her hiding place, raced across the floor and
leapt into my arms with a yelp of relief. She had come to stay.

From the start, she had class. When I described her as an
'aristocratic mongrel', I was only being factual—though there
was a touch of pride as well. She was spaniel-like, black, with the
gentlest eyes I have ever seen. There is the risk of making her
sound too good—she never yapped, and barked only on the right
occasions; she was obedient, though never cowered; she liked
everyone indiscriminately, but then she knew no fear. Above all,
she had gaiety. The man who said that dogs cannot smile, can
never have smiled himself. It is their capacity for joy that makes
me like all dogs, not only my own. I witness this in summer, with
the dogs on the beach below. On the hottest of days they are anxious to play, and if their owners are too occupied with the inertia
of sunbathing—stretched in rows like onions out to dry—the
dogs gallop off to explore. Smells and shapes are investigated,
other dogs greeted—at both ends—and then they are off in
sudden bursts of energy, zig-zagging across the sand in pursuit of
each other, or themselves. I suppose most animals experience this
abandonment—calves that skip along the skyline and lambs that
prance for the fun of it—but as they grow older they become
more staid. The dog is different. He is the only animal, not excepting man, that retains his innocence.

Littlewood became infinitely wise but never lost her playful-
ness. Though she was happy in the city, she possessed a wanderlust. Several times she escaped from The Waterman's Arms and
was noticed trotting off to the West India Docks to catch a ship
for some unknown destination. Anxious moments, with the roar
of dockland traffic, until she was recovered. This was her only
sign of dissatisfaction.

And then we moved. She settled here as if this were the place
she had been searching for all the time. I remember that once, on
Waterloo Station, a distinguished-looking man bent down to
stroke her. Lifting his tweed hat, he asked politely: 'And would
your little dog be a water dog?' I had never heard of the breed
before, but this is exactly what Littlewood would be. She swam
instinctively, following me so far out I would have to turn her

round, a wave washing her back to shore as if she was surfing. She would shake herself with apparent glee, and gallop along the edge of the water, her feathery tail waving high.

A stream runs down the ravine close to the house, and I used to refer to the 'pool' that we made by damming it, until I realised that people thought in terms of a swimming-pool. Anyhow, the pool, or puddle, was deep enough for Littlewood to dive into, and the fresh water made her coat more silky than ever. All water was irresistible: when it rained she sat on my balcony or on the wall outside, letting it soak refreshingly through her fur. But it soaked into her bones as well, and at one point she became so arthritic that she had to be carried. It was harrowing to see her inactivity. Then, miraculously, she recovered. Swims were discouraged now, but there were moments when the impulse could not be restrained and she would charge joyfully into the surf. I dried her down afterwards, a game she relished, biting the towel with pleasure, rubbing herself along the bed when I had finished. I had learnt, long ago, that it was either a tidy house or a home full of dogs. Littlewood also had the destructive urge to chew blankets, but as she did so from purest happiness when I returned from a journey, I found it hard to reproach her.

Towards the end of her life, when she was twelve or thirteen, Littlewood was grand and leonine, her fur bleached at the edges like a mane. There was a horrible moment when I found her with one eye exposed in red-raw flesh, after a fight or accident (I never discovered which) but skilful stitching by Mr Phillips, the vet, restored it perfectly, though at first the irritation was so acute that I fell asleep with my hand over her paws trying to stop her from scratching.

She reached an astonishing rapport with this place. As she became less energetic, she would lie on my balcony overlooking the sands, her nose twitching occasionally as she sniffed the breezes off the Atlantic. If she sighed, it was the sigh of deepest contentment.

Her sensitivity with me was absolute. The other dogs might clamber over a newspaper while I was reading it, or shove their noses against me demanding attention, but Littlewood knew the time for play and the time for rest. Her morning greeting was always a good-tempered start to the day, while her welcome after a long absence was so ecstatic I would have to calm her down. She would subside for a moment, even eye me reproachfully for having left her in the first place, but she could not endure such nonsense for long and jumped up again to lick me wildly in the happiness of knowing I was back.

And then she started to slow down. I wish it had happened more swiftly, yet it was over all too soon. I was faced with the familiar problem: was it crueller to lock her indoors or let her struggle to keep up with the others on the evening walk? One day she stopped in a nearby field and hurried back home with her tail between her legs and an expression of such distress that she might have seen a ghost—perhaps her own? Her limbs seemed to harden and this paralysis spread through her body until she was scarcely able to move and was carried upstairs at night. Mr Phillips had to be called out early one morning, for the last time. His verdict was no surprise: if she were allowed to live, she would suffer.

Littlewood knew. And with one final effort, for even this was difficult now, she managed to lick my hand in order to reassure *me*. Her eyes were dimmer but as generous as ever.

I left the room, and realised our long relationship was over.

Knowing the difference that a dog's companionship can make, I am bewildered by the present campaign—for this is what it amounts to—against dogs. All of a sudden they are declared a menace, the latest victims of our national hypochondria. A director general of a Government-sponsored Health Education Council has condemned the dog as 'a grubby bag full of germs', but I would rather touch a dog than a director general of a Health Council. A television doctor has warned parents not to allow their children to cuddle their dogs—tarnishing the most innocent of friendships—and a lady MP has recommended that we ban dogs from our beaches.

All this is done in the name of hygiene, which makes it appear to be in the public interest. The main objection is that dogs go about their business, to use one of those euphemisms. But what on earth did they do before? It is claimed that they pour 'a million gallons of urine' into the earth daily. At least that was the accusation in 1974 by the science correspondent of the *Sunday Times*, but there is inflation in all things and a lady reporter on television has announced that it is one *and a half* million gallons now. Still, it is a nice round figure. What I long to know is who measures it, and how?

Of course it is messy when dogs relieve themselves, though more natural than the poisoned wastes we empty into our rivers and coastline, and it would be commonsense to keep children's playgrounds separate. But there is a new scare—an eye disease that is undoubtedly nasty but so rare that many opticians are unaware of it, or would be if the risk had not been magnified out of all proportion. The danger lies in children sticking their fingers into dog's mess and licking them, a pastime parents would be wise to discourage anyhow. Then a virus can enter the bloodstream and damage the child's eyesight. Such an injury would be as tragic as a child's death by drowning, but it is no solution to ban either dogs or children from the seaside.

The bogey of rabies is largely responsible for the present panic, yet I would bet that more people will be killed by bumblebees than by a rabid dog. Death from rabies is virtually unknown in this country, unless contracted abroad. The Pasteur Institute has made the civilised comment that flu is more dangerous to the people of Western Europe, and you are more likely to catch a disease from your closest friend—human, that is.

With typical selfishness we are scared for ourselves. The real threat is to our wild life. It would be calamitous if rabies spread through our animals (dogs are not the only carriers, though you might think so from all the publicity) and upset the balance of our countryside. Of course every precaution should be taken, and penalties imposed on those who are silly enough to smuggle their dogs into Britain, but there is no reason for condemning dogs in general.

Are we becoming so coddled that we would prefer to curb our friendship with dogs rather than run any risk? Dare I say it: if someone dies from rabies, even if a child damages the sight of an eye, should we not accept this as one of the hazards of life? The present scare is a pathetic symptom of the urge to protect ourselves at all costs. We value ourselves too highly. The extinction of a species—be it as tiny a specimen as a blue butterfly—is a greater loss than the death of a thousand human beings. The shooting of the last rhinoceros would be more regrettable than the disappearance of a horde of *us* in an earthquake. There is this arrogant assumption that animals have been placed on this earth for our benefit. People seem more upset by dogs' mess on the pavement than by the laboratory tests on animals, performed on our behalf. Those figures are more horrifying than any risk of rabies; 5,397,084 experiments on living animals in 1975; 100,000 killed in our laboratories each week. And all for what? Not simply tests for cancer, but also for cosmetics; to make us not only feel better but *look* better. White rabbits are used to test shampoo, their eyes taped open sometimes with metal clips to stop them blinking; guinea-pigs have their fur stripped off with adhesive-tape so that the 'irritation' of after-shave lotion can be studied on their skin. The strength of weedkiller is tried out on animals until they die; dogs are forced to smoke, to test the effects of nicotine; bears are put in simulated car crashes. And these animals receive no relief.

I have been told that I care too much about such things, but the idea of an animal sacrificed in the cause of after-shave strikes me as the ultimate obscenity.

When I see the freedom of my own dogs, I am thankful for their happiness at least.

None of this explains how I came to possess eight dogs. It started with the absurd misjudgement that Littlewood needed a companion. Consequently, Sooty was picked from a squirming mass of black puppies with brown eyebrows in a box in Petticoat Lane one Sunday morning. She was chosen because she seemed the most lively, but this was soon revealed as a determination to look after herself. Sooty's philosophy was straight to the point: a full stomach and a good night's sleep. It was apparent at once, but too late, that the last thing Littlewood needed was a companion. She preferred the company of people to that of other dogs, whereas I prefer dogs to people. So Sooty was cast in the thankless role of unwanted friend, living in Littlewood's shadow, suffering from the comparison with this paragon. It is hardly surprising that she became increasingly ill-tempered until one day she bit Littlewood in the nose so sharply that one nostril remained dry for the rest of Littlewood's life. After that, each acted as if the other was invisible.

Sooty became more obstinate than ever, her expression permanently baleful, her days spent in indignation, barking at every passing car and even aeroplanes above. And then the whole point of acquiring her was lost, as Littlewood produced a litter of nine puppies by a whippet she had met in Hyde Park. From these we kept Pencil, all whippet except for lacking that whipped emaciation. Then Littlewood and Sooty went on a visit to Devon and were courted by Flash, the sheepdog belonging to Stanley Tucker's farm at Putsborough. They had their litters at much the same time, though Sooty was so unnerved that she dropped her puppies along the corridor and Littlewood had to feed them alongside her own. The new additions were Blacky and Bassey, and their half-sister Excellent.

From the moment we moved, the house seemed filled with puppies, until the dogs received regular injections from the vet. Excellent proved a perfect mother, in contrast to her own rejection by Sooty, and made a nest outside the house out of reach of the others. Her son, Muldoon, appeared on the West End stage as Crab in *Two Gentlemen of Verona* until he was knocked down by a Rolls Royce, and he is a familiar figure in Hampstead.

Pencil gave birth to a puppy who was never collected by the family that asked for her, and is known, consequently, as 'Puppy' to this day. Bassey had a daughter called Alice, too hysterical to be collected by anyone, and at that point I cried 'enough'. To my shame, I did not appreciate the ardency of Sooty's loyalty until it was almost too late. She became more intolerant, darting out at dustmen, growling at the butcher, resenting most people until Frances came to live here. If proof were needed that a dog can be transformed by receiving attention, Sooty provided it.

Frances and Sooty adopted each other instantly. At first Sooty was skittish, as if she reserved her last suspicions, but soon she trusted in her good luck and became blissful. Her morning treat was to drive to the village when Frances went shopping, sitting beside her in the front seat like a sportive grandmother. Somehow it seemed as if she were wearing a hat.

Her stamina became remarkable, as if she had gained a second childhood, as I am sure she had. On long walks around the nearby estuary, she would stride ahead while the other dogs panted behind. Once, when she saw us go out in the rowboat, she leapt from a top window on to the ground, raced across the sand, and swam out after us—or, rather, after Frances. They were so inseparable that Frances took the dog with her when she visited her father's home in Sussex. When the suitcases were brought out to the car, Sooty gave a look of dismay followed by a bark of delight as she was allowed to sit in the back, on her blanket. This was the first time she left Devon, but she adapted immediately at the other end so long as Frances was in sight.

When Sooty had to be left for a couple of hours one morning, it was simply because Frances had gone to the registry office where her father was being married for the second time. As she drove home, she found Sooty's corpse at the foot of the drive: she had been killed instantly by a passing car, having forced her way out in her determination to follow.

The grief can be imagined, but few dogs can have ended their days so happily. A true companion at last, she was fulfilled.

chapter four

The art of walking

I am not the sort of person who ends up in *Who's Who*, but if I were I should list my recreations as: talking to people in pubs; walking in silence with dogs. Walking for the pleasure of it is one of the most satisfying activities, mentally as well as physically. Sadly we seem to have lost the zest for it—yet another Victorian enthusiasm that a future generation will have to rediscover.

Charles Dickens thought nothing of striding home through the night from London to his home, Gad's Hill, near Rochester. When he attacked the hills of Cumberland, he urged his friend Wilkie Collins to accompany him: 'anywhere, take any tour—see anything'. He was fired by the idea of climbing 'a gloomy old mountain' called Carrock Fell, with a wretched guide and the exhausted Collins scrambling after him. When they reached the top at midday, a darkness fell like midnight and the guide confessed he did not know the way down. Such hazards are grist to the walker and Dickens was in his element, following a waterfall down the mountain on the assumption that it must lead to a river. There was a cry as Wilkie Collins slipped headlong and landed with a sprained ankle, but Dickens was equal to the mishap and heaved Collins over his back, carrying him the rest of the way while the sodden guide was dispatched for a dog-cart. Such activities were recorded under the surprising title *The Lazy Tour of Two Idle Apprentices*.

What fun they must have had! Imagine the relish of exploring Britain in the last century, with no cars, no telephones, no motorways and few people. And those welcoming wayside inns with log fires and warm punch that seem synonymous with Dickens, though I wonder how much his pen enhanced them.

My great-uncle Bram Stoker, the author of *Dracula*, was another insatiable walker. Literally a champion walker at Trinity College, Dublin, he was awarded silver goblets for winning 'the seven mile walking race' and for 'his gallant struggle in five miles walking'. Later, when he could snatch the time, he charged across the countryside as if he was seeking an outlet for surplus energy. The stamina of the Victorians seems inexplicable today: Bram Stoker ran several careers simultaneously, acting as manager of the Lyceum Theatre, writing several hundred letters a week in his own hand, arranging Henry Irving's tours of America and accompanying him, studying for the bar and passing—apart from writing eighteen books. Perhaps he felt a need to 'get away from it all', for instead of collapsing in a deck-chair in his spare moments, he set out at random, with a fine strong walking stick.

One August he set out from Peterhead to Aberdeen. After eight miles he came across the small herring village of Cruden Bay, where the Kilmarnock Arms made him welcome: 'When I first saw the place I fell in love with it. Had it been possible I should have spent my summer there in a house of my own, but the want of any place to live in forbade such an opportunity. So I stayed in the little hotel, the Kilmarnock Arms. The next year I came again, and the next, and the next . . .'

When I followed in his footsteps in 1970, I could understand his return to such tranquillity. The sands and inlets were the same as he described them in *Crooken Sands* and *The Mystery of the Sea*, though Slains Castle on the top of the cliffs, which was intact in his day, is a ruin now and truer to Stoker's gothic imagination, with open windows and broken archways looking out on the surf that lashed the rocks below. The Kilmarnock Arms still welcomed guests, but since my visit, North Sea oil has come ashore at Cruden and the population has leapt from a few hundred to several thousand.

More appropriate to this book was Stoker's discovery of Boscastle further down the coast in North Cornwall, which he 'hit on by accident' on an earlier walking tour. South of the flat and deadly resort of Bude, it is an exciting formation of land and sea with the incoming tide surging through the narrow opening, shouldering its way in as it fills the harbour. The current is so powerful that boats had to be winched in by cable, which must have appealed to Stoker. He wrote about the place so glowingly, transforming it into *Pencastle* in a short story about two fishermen in love with the same girl, and a corpse washed up by a storm on the hour of the wedding, that it became a fashionable holiday place for his friends—especially Henry Irving.

Today, Boscastle is a tourist attraction in the height of summer, with the inevitable car park and souvenir shop but the surprise of a Witches' Museum. Even so, it is not a place that can be easily tamed. The description of Boscastle as 'a veritable Venice of Cornwall' is utterly absurd for such a tempest-tossed shore: the sea fills and empties with a resounding roar into a hole known as the Blow Table or the Devil's Bellows; the Tower was built by revenue men to stop smuggling; and the jetty built in 1584 by Sir Richard Grenville provided the best anchorage along the coast when Boscastle was a busy little harbour where three-masted schooners and 200-tonners landed cargo. One ship, belonging to the wine merchants Rosevear and Sloggat, was chased by French pirates, who were astonished to see the vessel head straight for the rocks and disappear. Unaware of the invisible entrance, and thinking the captain had wrecked her deliberately, the French sailed off; the wine merchants built the Methodist chapel in thanks for Boscastle's deliverance.

The Cobweb Inn used to be the wine stores for Rosevear and

Sloggat, and blocks of iron from the Midlands steel works, carried as ballast, were used in the foundations.

In 1843 a gale ripped the roof off the Norman church and the priceless timbers were sold in due course for less than a pound a ton. At least some of the wood was acquired by Sir Henry Irving and carved into a stage 'throne' for the Lyceum Theatre. Horse-driven coaches reached Boscastle in 1853, when it boasted so many pubs that it was condemned as 'a filthy town', a description which must have been as wide of the mark as the comparison with Venice.

John Dyke, who edited *The Illustrated Lundy News*, now works for the National Trust in Boscastle and is the illustrator for this book. He sent me a pamphlet quoting a visit by two men in 1867 that suggests that some of the pubs were far removed from the gargantuan good cheer so often described by Dickens.

R. S. Hawker and his friend stayed at The Ship (known as the Atlantic House today) and were greeted by their hostess, 'a ruddy-visaged widow' called Joan Treworgy. She had been born two doors away and stayed within a range of five yards from her birthplace all her life, apart from a climb up the hill to Forrabury Church when she married. She was a large woman and when she led them into the 'parrolar' there was not enough space for anyone else. When they asked for separate rooms, there was consternation. She told them that all the gentry were accustomed to sleep 'two in a bed', and officers that travelled the country would do the same, but if they insisted she would do her best to manage it though they would have to pay. As for their request for dinner, they could have 'meat and taties. Some people call them "putra-ties" but we always say taties here'.

'In due time,' wrote Mr Hawker, 'we sat down in that happy ignorance as to the nature of our viands which a French cook is said to desire.' What a contemporary comment—how familiar that anticipation as you sit down to eat in France, the inevitable disappointment in Britain. The two men experienced the latter: 'It is a wretched truth that by no effort could we ascertain what it was that was roasted for us that day by widow Treworgy.'

'Boscastle baby?' suggested Mr Hawker. His friend ran out to the kitchen to ask the widow yet again, but returned with the unfailing answer 'meat and taties'.

Mr Hawker wondered *what* meat: beef, veal, pork? Curiously, there was not a vestige of bone, nor any recognisable shape. Years later he discovered the secret of their 'mysterious dinner'—*seal*!

But when they asked for their bill the next morning, the rough scribble on the kitchen bellows put them to shame:

	s	d
Captens T for 2	o	6
Sleep for 2	1	o
Meat and taties & bier	1	6
Bresks	1	6

'Four shillings and sixpence for bed and board for two wolfish appetites for a night and a day, to say nothing of the pantomime performed gratuitously . . . Good day, Mrs Treworgy! good day! "Tomorrow to fresh woods and pastures new"', and they continued their journey.

To walk from here to Boscastle for pleasure would be considered too arduous today unless you were something of a fanatic, and if work was involved it would be unthinkable. Yet there was a time when men thought nothing of walking tens of miles to work along this coastline, and perhaps we should envy them. In a charming booklet on Woolacombe and Mortehoe, *Two Villages*, R. F. Bidgood records that men still walked to work even after the arrival of the railway in 1875:

> One man, who worked on the making of the road known as the Marine Drive (from Woolacombe towards Vention), walked from Ilfracombe along the railway track down Sandy Lane to work every day. The working day was from 7 a.m. to 6 p.m. for 4½d an hour. The men asked for ½d an hour rise, and were given ¼d. A man who worked on this road said that at The Prince of Wales Pub at Ilfracombe 6d would buy: 1 pint of beer, 2d, 1 oz of tobacco, 3d, a box of matches, ½d, and there would be ½d change. A clay pipe was given away.

Men who worked for a Woolacombe builder would stay locally until the weekend. Then, after five o'clock on the

Saturday afternoon, they would stop work to walk via Challa-combe Hill to Crow Point beyond Braunton Great Field, and be ferried across the estuary to Appledore. From there they would walk to their homes at Bideford, and in some cases to Hartland. On Monday morning they returned to work, losing half a day's pay because of the distance they had to walk.

Builders would demand high compensation for such a journey today, but it must have been gloriously invigorating then—in any kind of weather. What better than the chance to explore your own country, but how many people would bother to do so now? Of the thousands who fly to Spain, how many would take the train north from London to Manchester just out of curiosity? Or leave the motorway to lose themselves deliberately? Or escape from the sleekness of city life and walk through the unspoilt countryside as the Victorians did?

Despite everything, the coastline north of Ilfracombe, relished by Hazlitt on one of his jaunts with Coleridge, remains aston-ishingly isolated. 'We walked for miles and miles,' he wrote, 'on dark brown heaths overlooking the Channel, with the Welsh hills beyond, and at times descended into little sheltered valleys close to the seaside, with a smuggler's face scowling by us, and then had to ascend conical hills with a path winding up through a coppice to a barren top, like a monk's shaven crown.'

The scowling smuggler is more likely to be a surly landlord, but you can make such a walk today. Lynton, or Linton as it was spelt then, and Lynmouth have always been separated from the rest of the country by the wilderness of Exmoor, apart from the time when they were connected to Barnstaple by the railway. They were places where people could escape from civilisation, and contemplate. Shelley rented a cottage there in 1812 and Southey wrote that it was one of the finest spots he knew.

Until Parliament commissioned John Loudon Macadam to superintend the roads in the Bristol area, there were dirt tracks where 'timid ladies' were seated on pillions 'clinging to the stal-wart forms of their male companions', with pannier-ponies struggling up the hills as they pulled a sledge resting on two poles like a cart in shafts, called a 'trackamuck'. The packhorses were described romantically as a cross between a moorland pony and a horse that swam ashore from the wreck of a ship in the Armada.

There were no cars and the only bicycles were penny-farthings; the best way to travel was on foot. As F. J. Snell exclaimed in his book, *North Devon:* 'Footing it is good, and some of the sweetest and most ravishing spots on the secluded coast must be left unexplored if the visitor refuse to avail himself of such powers as Nature has endowed him with.'

Encroachment came from the railway long before the insidious motor, yet, paradoxically, it preserved the countryside by carrying visitors direct to their destination instead of dispersing them all over the place with a network of roads. There may have been competitive reasons, but the railway enthusiasts regarded themselves as conservationists and opposed the link-up from Minehead to Lynton though it was intended exclusively for holiday visitors. A letter to *The Times* condemned 'the rude hand of the implacable engineer' and asked for help 'in calling the attention of all lovers of Exmoor and its stag-hunting to the danger which now threatens the spot in the shape of a projected "light railway" from Minehead via Porlock to Lynton. The proposed line would . . . cut through the coverts which are the favourite resort of the red deer.' A curious argument considering that they wanted to kill the red deer, but the letter continued blithely: 'One of the principle attractions of that district is that, without being really remote, it is in a greater degree than most holiday resorts exempt from the invasion of Saturday to Monday visitants, and accordingly the woods and paths still have their beauties.' The letter condemned the attempt by 'persons at a distance to turn to their own pecuniary profit the beauties and advantages of a district in which they have no interest whatsoever'.

Such highmindedness would have been more becoming if the opponents had not been the champions of the Lynton—Barnstaple Railway, particularly the magazine owner Sir George Newnes. This train service was opened on 11 May 1898, leaving Barnstaple at 11.15 a.m., with a fifteen-minute stop at Bratton where the *Yeo* led the carriages—four people on each side—through a triumphal arch and the parish council presented an address to Sir George. The journey came to a stop outside Lynton at 1.17 p.m., allowing Lady Newnes to alight and cut the red, white and blue ribbons stretched across the lines. After this they were entertained to lunch at the Valley of the

Rocks Hotel where Sir George made a speech expressing the hope that nothing would come of the Minehead line to Lynmouth 'as it would harm the beauty of the countryside'. In due course, he opposed it so strongly at a public enquiry that the plan was dropped.

To be fair, Sir George gave an annual prize of five pounds for the best-kept flower beds at the stations on the way, and expressed anxiety that his own line should not disfigure the 'Alpine villages'. Just as Boscastle was compared so ludicrously to Venice, Lynton and Lynmouth were dubbed the 'Switzerland of England', which seems incongruous for seaside villages dependent on herring. In order not to jeopardise the Swiss slopes, Lynton station was placed outside the village and passengers were met by horse-drawn coaches that took them down to Lynmouth on the *Zahnradbahn* through the pine trees.

In 1888 there had been three coach trips a day during the summer, twenty-seaters drawn by four horses, but the journey from Barnstaple to Lynton took close on three hours. The train took over. A sign outside the coach station in Joy Street recognised the transition with generous goodwill: 'Farewell ye coaches—success to the Lynton and Barnstaple Railway.' Mr Baker, the coach driver, became the station master at Chelfham where the elegant viaduct stands today.

But in their turn the motor-buses did the journey quicker and helped to kill the railway, though it ran for thirty-seven years. Third-class fares cost 3s 3d return and offered a daily service of three trains in winter and six in summer, even during the First World War. But competition from the car resulted in a decline from the 72,000 tickets sold in 1925 to less than half of that in 1932, and closure was announced. Lynton dignitaries made a last and desperate protest at a meeting with the local MP in Barnstaple, but destroyed their case completely by arriving in a limousine. The last train drew out on 29 September 1935 to the strains of 'Auld Lang Syne' and the next morning the station master placed a wreath on the stop-block at Barnstaple Town. The last locomotive was overhauled and shipped to Brazil, where it has been working ever since.

With a yearly loss of £50,000 there was no alternative, yet if the line existed today, especially if it was linked with Minehead, it would be a tourist attraction equal to that of Festiniog in Wales on which it was based, with the same 1ft 11⅝in gauge.

And so, in 1935, Lynton returned to the isolation of 'the English town farthest away from a railway'. It must hold this title with a vengeance today, now that the Taunton to Barnstaple line is closed and trains no longer run to Ilfracombe.

Again, it is the perfect jaunt for walkers.

I am lucky in the choice of walks around me though I have the discipline of eight wandering dogs unused to traffic. This means that I plan beforehand, to avoid as many roads as possible, climbing above the Marine Drive to the top of Potter's Hill to study the landscape. The drive was built for Miss Chichester, a local landowner whose family estate still owns Woolacombe Sands today. She drove along it in her carriage to admire the view and gave Potter's Hill to the public in 1935 to mark the Silver Jubilee of George V. R. F. Bidgood says it was named after Thomas Pottere in 1330, even though the shape suggests that it was moulded 'by a giant potter'. It looks over Woolacombe and Morte, and I made a note of gates and footpaths and possible short-cuts. It seemed straightforward until I started, when fields were revealed as bogs, and innocent fences were spiked with barbed wire to the top. After leading or lifting the struggling dogs round or over such obstacles, we reached a track on the other side of Woolacombe and climbed the hill, leaving the houses behind us. The dogs surged ahead scenting new pleasures, while I considered the best way of reaching Morte. We plunged into a wooded valley, with tall bare winter trees and banks covered with green ferns and ivy on either side of a tumbling stream. Streaker, the new dog belonging to Frances, disturbed a grey squirrel and the others followed her, howling in excitement over this new kind of rabbit. A bite away, and the honorary rabbit leapt up a tree and vanished, leaving them incredulous. After sniffing around frantically, they joined me gradually as I walked through a deserted caravan site, which I found surprisingly inoffensive. Usually I resent caravans because they are placed so conspicuously on the edge of the sea. They would not be so unlikeable if they were painted discreetly in camouflage colours of browns or greys, but they sit there, white lumps on the skyline, as if they are drawing attenion to themselves deliberately.

As with all development, what matters is not only what is done but *how* it is done. And this site could hardly be objected to, carefully placed so the caravans have splendid panoramic views of a valley, yet are virtually invisible. This is in line with the continental habit of concealing the sites rather than exposing them—a welcome antidote to our planners, who assume that everything must be made as easy as possible with the ultimate aim of dumping the car or caravan beside the sea so the people need never get out at all.

After crossing a lane and several stiles, I stepped back centuries. For the next two hours there was neither man nor car, though plenty of beasts—stupid scuttling sheep, staring wide-eyed cows, a nonchalant horse or two, and clattering pheasants that rose up right in front of me, flushed out by the dogs. To the right lay a deep, brown-ferned valley with a stream and a line of trees running along the bottom, towards Damage Bay. Judging by a signpost I had noticed earlier, the old farmhouse and out-buildings belonged to Easewell Farm, as comfortable as the name suggests.

Down a lane to Bull Point lighthouse. The tower was damaged in a recent storm but the new building blends with the old. The place seemed deserted, not that I wished to meet anyone. Instead I took the winding coast track beside Rockham Bay, hoping that Pencil would not flush a bird from the brambles and run after it, head in air, straight over the cliff. The coastal vessel *Stan Woolaway* sank at Rockham a few years ago and the Ilfracombe life-boat took off the crew. The American timber-ship *William Wilberforce* was one of the last to be lured to this bit of the coast, by wreckers in 1842. In the local tradition, a man tied a lantern to his donkey's tail to suggest a swaying ship and the helmsman thought he had plenty of water to move in. Six lives were lost and the figurehead of the schooner can be seen today on the *Cutty Sark* in dry dock at Greenwich.

Because of the wrecks, deliberate and accidental, a petition was sent to Trinity House in 1850, when five ships were lost in the first two months alone. Signed by merchants, shipowners and the local clergy, it asked that a lighthouse should be built because 'the barbarous conduct of lawless wreckers caused much loss of life and property'. That same year, the *William and Jane* of Barnstaple ran ashore at Barricane Beach and a woman carrying a heavy sack was noticed on the Morte road afterwards. She claimed it held wood, but a seaman's palliasse was found inside. R. F. Bidgood records that she was fined £1, but sentenced to twenty-one days in prison as she was unable to pay it: 'It is hoped that a little hard labour, with prison discipline, will warn her and others against such dastardly conduct in taking away from unfortunate mariners, especially those dead on the shore, any part of their property.' I should have thought that those 'dead on the shore' would have cared the least.

In 1861, on 1 January, the Spanish *Dulce Nombre de Jesus*, a beautifully constructed vessel of Spanish oak and copper, carrying a cargo of brown sugar, was wrecked at Rockham. Four sailors were drowned, including the Master, all from Bilbao; two more bodies were washed up on the beach and eight of the crew were saved. Apparently they climbed two masts at the height of the storm, holding on to the ship's rigging. The mast with the eight survivors fell towards the land; the other, with the six victims, towards the sea. There is a legend that when the villagers sorted through the wreckage they noticed a cushion lashed to a spar and a baby girl inside, still alive. She was taken to a farm called Damage Barton and adopted by the family, who gave her the name of Nancy. When she grew up she married the son of the family, but apart from references to a Spanish shawl and cushion, Mr Bidgood has not been able to verify the story further.

Finally, Trinity House took notice of the petition, and after considering Morte Point and Morte Stone, they built the lighthouse at Bull Point in 1879. But wrecks continue to the present day: one of the last was another Spanish ship, the *Monte Gerugu*, in 1949, when twenty-three survivors were rescued by the Ilfracombe lifeboat and two were washed ashore on the sands below and brought to this house by my father.

I finished my walk across these same sands, in the fading light. The dogs were fed, lying in assorted poses on my bed in front of the small open fire that I light in my bedroom when I am alone in winter. Bassey rolls on her back in one of her rare requests for affection. She has kept up admirably throughout the walk, for we must have gone fourteen miles or more and her legs are so weak that she needs help over stiles and fences. For a moment, I feel a twinge of guilt, suspecting I might have stretched her too far, but she looks content. And so am I, except for a nagging realisation that I am making too much of an uneventful day.

Another walk

A January day as radiant as this is worth a week of summer. Attracted by the name of Spreacombe, I started out past Pickwell Farm and the tall line of pines planted by Mr Parsons of the Croyde Post Office more than sixty years ago. In the summer this lane is used as a short-cut but there is seldom a car in winter, except for today when it resembled a minor motor rally with cars parked by the side with well-wrapped and binoculared riders inside. A suspicion that these were followers of the Dulverton Foxhounds was confirmed by a blast of hunting horns a few fields away and a glimpse of red coats on the skyline. As I stopped to talk to one of the drivers, a giant hare hopped over the hedge and sat in the middle of the road as startled as myself. Presumably the animal must have been alerted by the hunting hullaba-loo, but seeing the cars it decided it was safer to hop back again. Typically, the dogs failed to notice it—a fantasy unrealised. Walking on, I stopped at a low point in the hedge and looked over it to see the hare wriggling through the winter barley on her sto-mach. Perched on the road she might have been three feet high; now, when she stopped, a low molehill. I thought of leading the dogs into the field, but an image of them charging into the hunt encouraged me to walk on. Also, the hare was having enough to cope with, without such 'sport' on my part; it looked as if she was a doe, soon to give birth.

With various shouts, the fox hunters in the distance began to ride downwards to the sea. My feelings have changed towards them over the years. Once I thought the pursuit of any animal was indefensible, and still feel this where stag and badger and otter are concerned. But if foxes have to be kept down, I do not consider hunting worse than gassing. What irks me is the hypo-crisy that makes some hunt supporters claim the fox enjoys being hunted, instead of frankly admitting that they relish the glory of riding across the English countryside, the fun of dressing-up, the warmth of the stirrup cup. But even worse is the sour resentment of the protestors, who seem more anxious to prevent the hunters having a good time than concerned for the fox.

There are too many foxes around here, so I do not feel strongly either way. But I enjoy the rare glimpse of one as it trots sardonically across a ploughed field as if there were not a hound in the world, or peers round some gorse surprisingly close to home. Last year, a fire swept up the ravine above the sand dunes—the foxes' natural home. When I walked up there to inspect the havoc afterwards, I noticed a large dog-fox lying on the edge of the blackened scrub, wild-eyed, panting desperately, too exhausted to make a move, though it saw me. I thought of the wildlife choked to death in the fire, perhaps including his own vixen and cubs, and whistled to the dogs to follow me as we left the appalled animal alone.

Now, leaving the Dulverton Foxhounds to their pursuits, I felt inclined to wish the local foxes luck. This sentimentality was paid for, as I shall tell.

I continued to Spreacombe, crossing a field that skirted a dilapidated holding where Pencil found a scent that needed investigating and would not return until she was charged by a braying donkey, when she raced back swiftly. Three huge goats regarded us from a safe distance. Then we hit the lane that runs from Ox's Cross where Henry Williamson lives. Henry gave me a convincing explanation for the name: that this was a field of clover where oxen were rested for a couple of days to be fattened up on the way to the cattle market in Barnstaple; this accounts for the richness of his soil. But the signpost marks it as Oxford Cross, which seems illogical for a place so far from Oxfordshire and with little possibility of a ford at the summit of a hill.

I thought we would not meet a car, and I was right. I had not anticipated the beauty of the winter trees, their shapes are seen to perfection at this time of year, so striking that I stopped time and time again simply for the pleasure of studying them. Not just their delicate shapes, but their range of colour: deep pinks, greys, russet-browns and greens, one wood blending into another. They

were as magnificent in their height and number as any woodland
I have seen in Scandinavia, France or Austria.

A signpost with a bird, symbolising the Royal Society for the
Protection of Birds, identifies this stretch as Chapel Wood
though nothing remains of the chapel now, apart from a few
stones. With no idea how I would get back, I walked on, hearing
the noise of the main-road traffic from Braunton to Ilfracombe
come closer. I was relieved to reach Smallcombe Bridge, with
cows and calves standing in the water under the trees as if it were
summer. Then a turning left past the quarry, through Holts
Wood and Cleave Plantation, and up the hills past the simple,
white elegance of Spreacombe Manor. Then through two isolated farmsteads unmolested by civilisation, and again this feeling of elation that so much of this part of the world remains
unspoilt. Hens roaming free and deep mud everywhere, a distant
sound of cows and a dog barking, the only mark of the twentieth
century being a Jaguar car parked incongruously outside a barn,
a car with no wheels and a bashed-in bonnet; it could not have
been driven for years.

And so, after an hour, I struck the Georgeham road, and
headed down through the fields towards Vention. No sign of the
hunt, but as we reached the Grey House I saw the car and knew
that Peter and Frances had returned. The dogs recognised it too,
and charged ahead rejoicing.

JD

chapter five

The clash of two rivers

Driving to Braunton, the largest village in England, you turn inland after Croyde and meet the sweeping expanse of Saunton Sands. The view is so amazing, so bizarre, that people stop their cars to get out and stare.

It is a mixture of Egypt and Paradise—or so the film companies would have us believe. The sands were used as desert in Alexander Korda's *Caesar and Cleopatra*, and when the airman in *A Matter of Life and Death* recovered consciousness on the dunes, he thought he was in heaven.

Saunton Sands stretch for several miles, bending into the estuary where the rivers Taw and Torridge pour out to sea and clash whitely and often wildly at Bideford Bar. Behind the beach lie interminable sand-dunes that could stand in for the surface of the moon in yet another film, and behind these are the Braunton Burrows with flat marshy meadows, rushes and reeds, and the high nests of swans. If you are lucky you might spot a smooth, brown, baby otter. There are 3,000 acres altogether, privately owned by the Christie Estate.

In the ice age the sea was thirty feet higher; as the ice moved rock and granite from Scotland it receded, leaving a shingle beach, and then the first and biggest sand-dunes along the western coast. Then a skin of vegetation stabilised the sand and prevented further erosion inland. That was 2,000 years ago. Later, Dutch engineers drained the ground to provide some of the finest cattle-fattening marshland in Britain. Today there is a new threat of erosion with a daily invasion of 800 cars in summer, and a desperate attempt by conservationists to stabilise the sand by planting marram grass. Until twenty-five years ago, such work was done by amateurs; now there are nature reserves set up by the government.

With characteristic British compromise, the Burrows are a reserve for wild flowers: sea stock, viper's bugloss, and the orchids that flower after a spring rainfall; yet also a training-ground for the army. Signs placed side by side warn you not to go within firing-range when the red flags are flying, and ask you not to destroy the wildlife. Against all logic, but as so often with British compromise, this seems to work, with army engineers helping to build an observation tower for bird-watchers.

The Burrows were famous for birdlife, and may be again. There used to be flights of geese, heron, and three thousand oyster catchers. But rare species, like the kestrel, have been shot and others vandalised—recently nine nests of swans were destroyed, pointlessly. An additional hazard were the jets of the Royal Air Force that skimmed above you as they took off and landed at Chivenor air base on the other side of the Braunton River, known locally as the Braunton Pill. But changes can be beneficial, and in 1970 Chivenor was closed down and the RAF, like the Clovelly herring, moved elsewhere. As the warning flags of army manoeuvres are rare, and the sound of firing rarer, this is now one of the most peaceful places you can find in England.

If you go there by car, you drive out of Braunton to the toll gate which is everything a country toll should be, with an old thatched cottage, a tousled sheepdog, ducks on a stream, and a gracious lady who comes out to bid you good morning as she opens up the gate, after she has first extracted your ten pence.

The Pill flows to the left. I moored a boat there and have happy memories of navigating the twists and turns of the river—deceptively shallow until it enters the estuary. Even now, there are masses of birds on the mud-flats at low tide. A rare ibis returned inexplicably every spring until last year, either a refugee from an aviary in a zoo, or, more romantically, flown all the way from Egypt. Perhaps, like the kestrel, it has been shot by someone.

You drive on past dykes and ditches and small rough farm sheds until you reach the solitary white house that was so lonely once, but now looks over the estuary to the vast power station opposite. Yet, because it is unpretentious, a functional building like the covered shipyard at Appledore, this is less offensive than one would expect. More distressing to me, having enjoyed so many picnics beneath it as a boy, is the loss of the old lighthouse near the Bideford Bar. There was a real house below the light, and I enjoyed the fantasy of living there in solitude. It was replaced by an uninteresting automatic light, and now even this has gone, replaced in its turn by the tower for bird-watchers. On an average day there are 27,000 birds on the estuary.

It is a memory now, but the estuary was once alive with shipping too, not merely busy but gloriously so. It seems inconceivable today but even Braunton boasted a bustling port at Vellator where the River Caen joined the Knowle to form the Braunton Pill. The Caen was named by William Grenville, who received land from his cousin, William the Conqueror, and came from Caen in Normandy, while 'pill' is a local word for a small river or creek. Pilton at Barnstaple is literally 'the town on the pill' though I flinch from the interpretations that might be given today!

As I am name-dropping, I should mention that Braunton takes its name from St Brannock, who came from South Wales to convert the Britons in 550. When the church he was erecting on the hill collapsed, he heard voices telling him to build another where he saw a sow grazing with seven piglets. Such a sight cannot have been rare, and it was not long before he sighted a sow and her litter in the meadow below. The church stands there today with a pig and piglets carved into the roof. A bench inside has the carved figure of Sir John Schorne, an eccentric who passed himself off as a parson from Buckingham-shire and claimed he had tamed the devil. To prove his assertion he had concealed in his shoe a wooden devil that would pop up briefly when he released it by pressing a spring in his heel. The devil was plainly in the parson's power—the original 'Jack in the Box', or so it is claimed. The carved figure here shows the devil in a cup rather than in the boot.

There were three limekilns at Vellator, where farmers com-peted to buy slaked lime, and ships up to 200 tons brought coal from South Wales to be sold for sixteen shillings a ton. One ship brought dried cod across the Atlantic from Newfoundland. When they were empty the ships were laden with iron ore from the mines at Spreacombe, or taken to Fremington to carry china clay to Gloucester. They were sailing ketches of course, with names like *Bessie Gould* and *Fishguard Lass*, and the sailors who manned them had names still famous in the district today: Chugg, Butler, Chichester, Tucker.

Braunton Pill flows surreptitiously into the Taw (meaning 'water'), which flows fifty miles from Dartmoor to the sea. The sponge-like peat of the moors acts as a reservoir, supplying a con-stant flow of water all the year round, though you would hardly have thought it in the autumn of 1976 when householders were forced to queue with their buckets—as daft an example of bureaucratic incompetence as can be imagined.

Barnstaple on the Taw was the leading port in the South West. Boutport Street was literally 'about port', though one his-torian claims that 'port' is another word for 'staple', or the ex-clusive market that gave the town its name.

Inevitably this part of England is linked with the Armada, but Barnstaple was adventurous before that. The second expedition fitted out by Sir Walter Raleigh and his cousin Sir Richard Gren-ville left Barnstaple in 1586, destined for America and the new state of Virginia, which Raleigh had named after Elizabeth, the Virgin Queen. But Bideford Bar proved insuperable. As the town clerk recorded: 'On April 16th, Sir Richard Grenvylle sailed over the Barr with his flee boat and friget, but for want of suffict water on the barre, being neare upon neape, he left his ship.' This proved a direct cause of the disintegration of the first

English settlement in America, for the colonists were so discouraged when no ship arrived to relieve them that they seized the chance to sail home in a barque of Sir Francis Drake's which was returning to England after the sacking of St Domingo. Reaching Portsmouth later in the year, they must have passed Grenville, who arrived to find the colonists gone. He left fifteen men, but 150 emigrants sent by Raleigh the following year learnt that they had been killed by the Indians or driven away. Grenville was preparing a further fleet in 1588 when he received orders from the Privy Council to hold back to meet an emergency—the Spanish Armada.

There has been rivalry over the parts played respectively by Barnstaple and Bideford, a rivalry confused by Kingsley's fictional claims for the latter in *Westward Ho!* But it seems that the squadrons of Raleigh and Grenville were the same as the ships that sailed from Barnstaple Quay. According to the town clerk, five ships sailed from Barnstaple over Bideford Bar to join Drake at Plymouth: the galleon *Dudley*, the *God Save Her*, the *Tyger*, the *John* (which was paid for and supplied by local merchants, a common form of defence at that time), and a fifth, unnamed ship.

The *Tyger* was probably Grenville's ship, while the *Dudley* was a Spanish ship brought to Barnstaple in 1586 and renamed by Raleigh as a calculated compliment to Robert Dudley, Earl of Leicester.

After the great naval victory, Barnstaple was rewarded when 'reprisal ships' seized gold from Spanish galleons, one of which was brought to Barnstaple Quay in 1592 with prizes worth £10,000, a fortune then.

There was further prosperity when Huguenots fled from persecution after the Edict of Nantes was revoked in 1685. Eight Barnstaple ships, importing wool from the trading centre of Rochelle, returned with 126 French refugees who arrived in Barnstaple on a Sunday to be welcomed with food and shelter from the residents. Their hospitality was repaid, for the Huguenots were outstanding weavers and brought all their skill and knowledge to the local wool industry.

Barnstaple was rich and the riverside was lined with the splendid houses of the merchants. Most of these have been destroyed, one of the finest to make way for a post office. An early lithograph shows how delightful the quayside must have been when there were benches on the cobbles outside the Star Inn with the colonnaded Exchange at the end of Queen Anne's Walk. There was a Nayle Stone where money was placed to seal a bargain, hence the saying 'paid on the nayle', and a statue of Queen Anne given to the town by Robert Rolle MP: it weighed two tons and rested on a pedestal with carvings by Caius Cibber underneath. This pedestal was nineteen feet from the ground, supported by central pillars and Tuscan columns on the side, and royal birthdays were celebrated by the mayor and corporation who drank wine and ate Barnstaple Crisp Cake underneath while nuts and sweets were handed out to the children. The Exchange is a building to be treasured.

Astonishingly, it stands there still, though it might as well be rubble for all the advantage that is taken of it. Far from being the focus of the town, it is backed by other buildings that obscure its outline. As for the Strand, which could be such a spacious promenade beside the river, it is dominated by a bus stop. Now a £9,000 'improvement plan' is promised, or threatened, complete with discreet directional signs and a renovated bus station. There will be no 'encroachment' on the Strand flower gardens but these are hardly inspiring as they are. With the old railway station of Barnstaple Town lying derelict around the corner, where buses could turn to their drivers' content, a dreamer is needed rather than a planner.

At times it seems that town councils are ashamed of the older parts of their towns, or obsessed with their own plans—which can look so impressive on paper yet so shoddy in reality—or blinded by self-interest. Fortunately, they have left Bideford Quay alone and it is possible to imagine the loveliness of the town described in the opening words of *Westward Ho!*: 'All who have travelled through the delicious scenery of North Devon must needs know the little white town of Bideford, which slopes upwards from its broad tide-river paved with yellow sands, and many-arched old bridge where salmon wait for autumn floods, toward the pleasant upland on the west. Above the town where the hills close in, cushioned with deep oak woods, through which juts here and there a crag of fern-fringed slate; below they lower, and open more and more in softly-rounded knolls, and fertile squares of red and green, till they sink into the wide expanse of hazy flats, rich salt marshes, and rolling sand hills, where the Torridge joins her sister, Taw, and both together flow quietly towards the broad surges of the bar, and the everlasting thunder of the long Atlantic swell. Pleasantly the old town stands there, beneath its soft Italian sky, fanned day and night by the fresh ocean breeze, which forbids alike the keen winter frosts, and the fierce thunder heats of the midland; and pleasantly it has stood there for now, perhaps, eight hundred years, since the first Grenville, cousin of the Conqueror, returning from the conquest of South Wales, drew round him trusty Saxon serfs, and free Norse rovers with their golden curls, and dark Silurian Britons from the Swansea shore, and all the mingled blood which still gives to the seaward folk of the next country their strength and intellect, and, even in these levelling days, their peculiar beauty of face and form.'

Reading such words, many must have yearned to visit the little white town and it is right that a statue at the end of the quay should commemorate the author. It is claimed that he wrote part of *Westward Ho!* at the Royal Hotel, originally a merchant's house built in 1688. You can see the upper room where he worked, perfectly preserved, with a magnificently decorated plaster ceiling and a wreath of flowers in relief. It conveys, instantly, the style in which the richer merchants lived and the brilliance of their taste.

The other great attraction of the town is Bideford Bridge with twenty-four arches spanning the Torridge. Constructed from oak in 1300 it was rebuilt with stone in 1460 and repaired after floods a few years ago without much loss of character.

Sir Richard Grenville was born in Bideford in 1541 and it was largely due to his colonisation of Virginia and Carolina, and the establishment of the tobacco trade, that the town became prominent. By 1570 fifty ships sailed to the Newfoundland Banks every year and by 1680 Bideford was by far the most important port in North Devon and the quayside was built that is still so attractive today. By this time Bideford monopolised the tobacco trade importing more leaf in 1700 than any port in Britain, not excepting London, and needing twenty-six customs officers to cope. It has been said that Bideford was the third most important port in the country a hundred and fifty years ago, and though this seems exaggerated the boast gives an idea of the town's reputation. When Kingsley arrived there, four sailing boats were making regular passages to America taking emigrants from 'the old country' to the new.

Gradually the cargo became more mundane—coal, timber, cement—but as late as 1951, 44,000 tons of goods were discharged on the quay and shipping in the estuary was still enough to justify three lifeboats working from Appledore before the bar. One of these was kept inside a boathouse on Braunton Burrows, a mile from Saunton. It started service in 1912, but as the Appledore crew were called out by the lighthouse keeper at Braunton, had to be ferried across to Crow Point, and then ran two miles to the lifeboat, which was dragged to the raging surf by a team of eight to twelve horses, it is hardly surprising that it closed down seven years later. Even so, in spite of the delay, the Saunton lifeboat saved eighty-three lives and one night it took forty sailors from the four-masted vessel *Penthesilia*, which had been driven on to Saunton Sands. In 1923, a hospital hulk was kept at Crow Point to keep in quarantine yellow-fever suspects from the entering ships; that has gone too, with less regret.

If you are unable to explore the estuary by boat, do so on foot. I leave the car beyond the bulb-farm and walk with a couple of the dogs up the road made by the American army in the last war. It's ravaged now by pit-holes, though the occasional amphibious tank might lumber past, apparently unseeing, like a prehistoric monster.

Always the contrast of the West Country: the tors of Dartmoor in the far distance, a smouldering blue on some hot days, stretching from undulating fields with the Great Field of Braunton right in front. Covering 360 acres, this was cultivated in the medieval strip system as early as 1325, with approximately 400 strips in 1890. Villagers had the traditional right to glean the ears of corn left lying after the final harvest, cut by hand with sickles.

Today there are fewer than a dozen farmers, using mechanical harvesters and binders. At least the parish council of Braunton has saved the Great Field from falling into the hands of developers, even though Whitehall has refused to schedule it for protection. Yet again this wilful short-sightedness, which considers a housing estate more important than the finest example of ancient strip farming left in England.

Nearing the estuary, a wooden track—made recently by the army from old railway sleepers to prevent erosion from too many wandering footsteps in summer—veers to the right. The dunes rise around one and the perspective is odd with peaks and depressions.

The path is helpful, but there is no indication where it leads until you breast a sudden slope—and there is a glorious panorama over the battered breakwaters below to Appledore across the water and the Pebble Ridge of Northam Burrows, with the white waves of Bideford Bar and the ships waiting outside to ease their way in when the tide is high.

It is the tide, of course, that provides the constant surprise. As it rises, every sort of coaster, ketch and fishing boat sails by, often black silhouettes against the shimmering water, passing shapes on a silver background.

At low tide, men fill their cement barges at Crow Point with sand and gravel which they carry later down the Pill, so overladen that the deck is almost level with the sea. To an alien eye, they threaten to sink at any moment.

I returned to this scene one September a few years ago, after a holiday at St Tropez. Every day had been perfect: we swam and ate our lunch in the sun and basked in it afterwards, but every day had been the same. Returning here, watching a falling raspberry sun transform the landscape in a series of fire-like flashes, turning it black, silver and scarlet, I realised how blessed we are in the subtlety of our light. I was aware, as I had not been for the past two weeks in the Mediterranean, that the light in England does not remain the same for a single day or hour.

This bend of the estuary never disappoints. No wonder that early travellers stayed to build a settlement among the sandhills. Two hundred years ago, the remains of St Ann's could be seen, a small chapel measuring $14\frac{1}{2}$ ft high, by 12 ft. But the stones were taken away for cowsheds and the ruins gradually disappeared. There is a pleasing theory that Crow Point took its name from the picture of the raven decorating the pennants of Hubba the

Dane when he landed here, thankful to find such a sparkling haven in a strange land.

Though peaceful, the scene is one of constant activity. Fishermen in high white waders haul their encircling salmon nets, known as 'seines', with floats on the surface and weights below; gulls prise mussels free from their clusters, and fly to a great height to drop them onto rock below to break their shells; oyster catchers cry wistfully and continually; a crowd of black cormorants lines the edge of the water, resembling a row of unctuous ushers waiting for a funeral; they take off like swans when I come close, disturbing the sea, which has been as translucent as an arctic lake at the lowest moment of the tide.

I have come to the edge to pick mussels, another incentive for visiting the estuary. My youngest dog, Bonzo, Bassey's granddaughter, is dismayed as she tries to scramble after me over the banks of sharp broken mussel shell: they must feel like a million blunt razor blades to her. She gives up and races off to make sure the others are all right. I can see Peter fishing in the far distance. A short while later, when I am in the mussel beds, I hear a strange sound—some army siren, perhaps—and straighten up to listen. It is no siren, but Bonzo squatting on a distant sandbank and howling with discontent. The sound is so forlorn that I hasten back, having collected all the mussels I need. She jumps up with delight and dashes off again, to check on the others. She is most concerned about everyone and everything.

How odd the British are in their suspicion of mussels; how wise the French to prize them as delicacies. They are not 'a poor man's oyster' in any way, but a versatile shellfish in their own right, providing the simplest yet most magnificent of soups, *moules marinière*. Unlike the oyster they are eaten boiled, and these on the estuary are cleansed by two fierce tides—they could hardly be less contaminated.

I collect them on good days for the fun of it, and for the satisfaction of eating them later. There are others along this coast who collect shellfish for a living. Sadly, they are a dying race.

The shrimper

Brendon Sellick is a shrimper with a hundred nets stretched

across the mud flats of Bridgwater Bay. He may well be *the* shrimper, the last of his kind. This is not surprising, for his life is tough by the standards of today. To cross the interminable mud, he uses a wooden sled that he calls a 'mud horse', sliding it across the surface. Though it may look easy, the vital balance is acquired only through experience.

'Do you go out every day?' I ask him.

'We go out for ten days on the trot. Then we get three or four days off because the tide doesn't come back far enough to uncover the nets.'

When they are uncovered, an average catch is 75 per cent small brown shrimps, with the remainder made up of sprats, mullet, bass, plaice, dover sole, whiting, cod and conger—also caught in the mesh. Brendon gathers them during the couple of hours when the tide is low and sorts them out when he returns home. After encouraging the boiler to a fierce red glow, he throws the shrimps into an old-fashioned fourteen-gallon copper, where they turn pink. When the tide is wrong, or the weather too wild, he repairs his nets in his farmhouse—a constant need after the storms.

'How many men are there along the Bristol Channel who make their living solely from this sort of fishing?'

'There's only two of us left now. There were three families two years ago, and there used to be dozens around the Bridgwater estuary, but it's died out now.'

'Why did they give it up?'

'I suppose they found easier ways to make a living.'

'Have you ever thought of giving up?'

'Not really. I've never done anything but this. I was brought into it, and my father all his life, and my grandfather. Never did anything else. We've been doing it for generations. And we've used the same old system, the mud horse, to get us across the flats—we've used that for hundreds of years. We did try a mechanical thing, but no success at all. We got it from Sweden, but it only lasted a matter of weeks.'

'What went wrong with it?'

'Useless in the mud; the mud just grinds into everything. Six hundred pounds thrown away.'

'I see you have snow-shoes hanging on the wall outside.'

'Ah, that's only when we get a lot of snow in. But they are not very successful on the mud, no. It varies from a foot to six or seven feet, even deeper in places.'

'So you could sink right in?'

'Oh yes, you could do. This is the idea of the sledge, you see, you slide across the top and it's surprising what weight you can carry—you can put three. or four or five hundredweight and push across.'

If the loss of £600 for the 'mechanical thing' suggests rich rewards, this is misleading. No man would undertake such work for financial gain. Brendon Sellick is a man content with his work despite the dreariness of this part of the coastline and the bitter cold in winter. 'We've got a job to keep up with most people today, but we still manage to. Whether we will be able to always, I don't know. I hope so.' Though it would seem a monotonous existence to many people, better to read about than do, Brendon sees it differently: 'It's pretty tough, but the satisfying part is when you go out and get a good day's catch, a good day's pay, like. It's so unusual, you go out today and not much, and then the wind turns round and you have a damned good catch—a really lovely lot of eels and plaice. It's so uncertain, you don't know from one day to the next what you are going to get.'

'And the really cold, dark winter nights, do you dread going out?'

'No, not really. I like it in the cold weather, as long as it's not freezing too hard, 'cos if it's freezing it kills the shrimps before we can get them out of the net. But on ninety days out of a hundred it's all right.'

Brendon hopes that his son Adrian, who is twenty-one and helps him in the summer, will carry on after him. 'It's up to him of course, but I think he will take to it. He seems to like it now anyway. He's gone to work now, just for the winter, but I expect he'll be back again in the early spring when the weather's nice.'

'So it might be Sellick & Son yet again?'

'Yes. I can just remember my grandfather. He used to take me as a little boy down to the beach to meet my father coming in from the fishing.'

'Was it different then?'

'Not really. I think they used to catch a lot more, but of course they never used to get the money for it.'

'What about pollution today?'

'It doesn't affect us in the channel as much as it does up the river, then it gets worse and there's some chaps that catch salmon up there and in the last few years it's been awful for them. But I think they're getting on top of this pollution—things might get better rather than worse. So long as we keep catching a fair amount each day, then you can live all right.

'This is my life, and I don't think I'd like to do anything else, not now. Sometimes I think I'd like to earn a bit more money and buy a few more things, but not really. If I won the pools, I'd still carry on doing this for the rest of my life, I'm sure.'

'You're a man in love with his work?'

'Oh not half, yes! And I wouldn't be able to do any other job. For one thing, I eat an awful lot of fish. It would be hard to get that anywhere else, wouldn't it? I eat a lot of eels: I like jellied eels and stewed eels and fried eels. I love them, you know. And dover soles, but I prefer the eels to the soles!' He glows at the thought.

'What of your family? Do they have to eat fish, or do they like it too?'

'They all like fish. And we have two pigs, and milk from the goat only she's dry at the moment.'

And a pony, and two dogs, and six girls, and one handsome son, and a lovely wife. Oh lucky man!

The mussel man

As Brendon Sellick is the shrimper of Bridgwater Bay, Brian Hill is the mussel man on the Taw and Torridge Estuary. What I do for the sake of my *moules marinière*, he does in earnest. Like Brendon he fulfils a family tradition, though his father saw no future in such fishing and insisted that he learnt his trade as a carpenter.

'He tried to put me ashore to give me a better standard of living, but I didn't like it and returned to fishing. It's all right, you've got nobody governing you, it's just your own way of life.' At least his apprenticeship taught him enough to build his own boat, which he takes out from the creek at Muddlebridge near his home at Fremington. Brian Hill is one of thirty-six men—'far too many part-time fishermen'—who have £20 licences to fish the river. Though they are becoming scarcer, salmon still swim up to the creek and he points to the spot, as we putt-putt under an old railway bridge, where he caught a twenty-two pound salmon in his nets not long ago.

Fish provide his main income in summer, but in winter he concentrates on the mussels. He is exceptional here in owning his mussel beds. 'I have my own part of the river, you know. To lay the beds you get the smallest spat mussels, take them out and drop them where they should mature properly, and then you harvest them. It's the fat content, you see—you can have a good-sized shell but the content inside may be very low because it came from the wrong spot.'

'How do you know the right spot?'

'Experience. It's not always the same spot every year.'

'Do you put them near sewage?' I ask, idiotically.

'Oh God, no!' Brian gasps.

Owning stretches of the river, he is covered by 'orders' that give him the right to lay the mussel beds, and no one else can pick them there. Few people would want to. Expense-account diners in smart city restaurants can have little idea of the effort and energy that goes into providing their *moules*.

I have watched Brian Hill, with his alarming, jagged rake, the long handle made from an old stair bannister, dredging the beds underneath the power station across the estuary from the White House. It may be because of the discharge of warmer waters that the mussels are especially large here. One aspect of mussel-picking still baffles me: those vast half-empty shells, twice the size of any full mussel I have ever found, as if discarded from a giant's dinner. Where have they been when full? Tantalising.

After comparison, you can tell the best mussels by the colour—a deep purple. Hill uses a rake because these beds are seldom exposed, even at the lowest tide, and he brings the mussels up in clusters, discarding any that are broken, throwing the biggest into a corner of the boat, letting the smallest fall through the mesh in his sieve to return to the river-bed for re-seeding. Altogether the mussels take a fair amount of punishment: Hill jumps around on top of them, and when they are stored in sacks he leaves them on the shore of the creek for several days, barely covered by the two tides, which suggests they can stand tougher treatment than people think.

The pearls he finds inside the shells are too small to be of value, but his rake has picked up an anchor, and an outboard motor that still worked until the owner arrived to claim it.

'What is the strangest catch you've ever had?'

'Oh, many things. The salmon that caught itself, I should think. It jumped into the boat.'

'Did it jump out again?'

'Not likely!'

Like Sellick, Hill goes out in all weathers and sometimes he is lucky to return. 'When the wind veers from the south to the north-west, you get it very bad then.' I ask if he has ever been scared, when rough weather hit the estuary.

'Two or three times' he admits. 'I got a rope round my leg on one occasion, and I'm near enough going over the side with it, on the anchor. I couldn't walk for a week after that.'

'How did you save yourself?'

'I just managed to hold on to the front of the boat, you know. Otherwise, once you're over the side you'd be drowned.'

'No chance?'

'Not when you've got a rope round your leg and the weight of the tide is against you, you're absolutely trapped, and that's it.'

It is feet rather than hands that suffer from the cold, from standing still so long: 'You get chilblains so you can hardly walk.' And there have been times when an office job in town has tempted him; 'Shouldn't like it in the summer though. Don't know that I should like it in the winter, really. I might do, as I get older.'

I think of the good times I have enjoyed on the estuary, but I wonder if it is ever fun for him: 'Of course it is, you'd never stay at it else, would you! It's always got its moments, every job has. I could be accused of being on holiday in the summer.'

'What is your philosophy in life? Being on the water like this gives one a great feeling of solitude, and time to think.'

'Yes,' he agrees, 'I think a lot. The main thing really is to make just enough money to keep going and do what *you* want to do, rather than be forced around like the rest of the people. I mean, they don't do a job because they want to do it, but just for the financial reward, and that's it.'

'But I think there's a yearning for this style of open life today.'

'I'm sure of that, but there again I think that as everything gets industrialised, this sort of life is being killed. It's dying slowly. It's got to be.'

'Why has it "got to be"? Are the pressures that great?'

'The pressures are too great. You've got more sewage—if they kill off the top waters where the fish are spawning, obviously you won't get the same number of fish here, not in the end. It's the industrial waste that does the damage, not the human beings so much.'

There are still a few men in the West Country who comb their own mussel beds at Teignmouth and Port Maddock, but it seems probable that in fifty years' time the ways of life enjoyed by Brendon Sellick and Brian Hill will be memories.

Brian Hill suspects he is the last of his line and doubts if his son will follow him; 'Still, my father said that about me and put me out to do a trade, and I came back. Who knows?'

When I ask about the appeal of such a life to young people, he shakes his head: 'I think the only people you will get doing it in a few years' time will be those drawing dole on national assistance.'

He overrates their stamina. I doubt if they would welcome the cold and foggy mornings as he does, 'when you can hear where you're going by the noise of the water and the birds'.

chapter six

West Country writer

My happiest memory of Henry Williamson is a picnic we enjoyed underneath the site of the old lighthouse on the estuary in the summer of 1975.

Unlike the endless summer of '76, the day was hot but invigorating, hazy without the glare. The Burrows retained the freshness of spring and, as we walked along the lanes, Henry pointed to the parts of the landscape that he has described so vividly in his books. If you have not read them, you have much to look forward to—the lean splendour of his prose, and his unique record of life in the West Country. In years to come, this part of the world will be measured by his words.

Describing the peaceful days between the two wars, Williamson writes of a simpler life that can never return. We tend to think of 1914 as the great watershed of changing values, but 1939 may prove equally cataclysmic. Even so, the motor-car was starting to invade our countryside long before Hitler thought of doing so. Henry makes this startling reference to Vention (in *The Children of Shallowford*):

> The sands were not what they were; more and more people were to be seen on them. On some days of August we passed as many as three or four cars standing in the rocky gateway near the top of the steep lane leading down to the old lime-burners' cottages. And on the sands themselves, often a dozen people beside myself were bathing. The place was spoiled.

Spoiled! Three miles of sand and a dozen people—in August!

Yet even I remember sitting against the rocks near our wooden steps in summer, listening to the flow of my father's enthusiasm, noticing my mother's dismay when figures appeared on the beach and approached too close. I feel sure she murmured 'Blackpool'. What would she have thought of the people-peppered sands today, so dense in August that it is hard to find an open space to swim? As for the three or four cars, there can be a thousand in the car park on a summer's day now, and the lane is so blocked that it is impossible to drive against the tide of traffic at the wrong hour. But all is relative; perhaps even this will seem unspoilt one day.

Henry zoomed into the tranquillity of Georgeham on a brand new Norton motor-bike in 1920. He had been staying with his parents in Lewisham and had been 'living it up' in London, climbing through his bedroom window at two in the morning, until his father cried out: 'You're killing me. I don't know if you're ill, but you've got to leave home.'

Henry was suffering from the reaction to his experiences in the First World War. He was one of that band of men whose lives would never be the same afterwards, not just because of the horror and the holocaust but because it was a shared, and in some ways a noble, experience, which could never be recovered.

In the novel *The Dream of Fair Women*, young Willie Maddison comes to North Devon, just as Henry did, in search of solitude. But he remembers the wartime days with a regret that is wistful:

> Never again to have such friendships? Or to see the white flares beyond the parapet at night and hear the mournful wailing of gas horns over the wastes of the Somme battle-fields? Gone, gone for ever. His heart ached: the splendid bitter days of the war dimmed the sunlight as he lay on the beach of shells, among the dried weed and black brittle cases of dog-fish eggs cast up during old storms.

The village of Georgeham, which is still so gentle, provides the antidote. He calls it 'Ham' in his books, and describes how he lived there for the next four years in a cottage beside the stream and next to the church, with walls a yard thick and a white owl in the thatched roof above. He rented it for five pounds a year.

The mood of contentment had remained with him during the days and weeks that followed, while he revised his manuscript, and walked many miles every day, arising with the sun and sleeping dreamlessly. He bought the spaniel pups from Brownie, and carried home two kittens with them; and finding a seagull with a broken wing, on the shore, he took that too. Very soon he had an otter cub, and various fledgeling birds, a buzzard hawk, carrion crow, jay, magpie, and jackdaw.

Leaving the village after breakfast, Maddison/Williamson—the two are inseparable—takes this entourage to a shell-beach near Baggy Point:

> The otter cub slid into the fresh water, rolling and swirling, biting the bubbles as it played on its back, while the jay, the crow, the hawk and the jackdaw, flew round Maddison's head, screaming for their breakfast.

Moving to a roomier cottage fifty yards away, Henry wrote fiercely into the night by candlelight, his baby son often cradled in the curve of his left arm. Though he failed to find the permanent solace he was searching for personally, he found himself as a writer. Inspired by the otter cub that had visited the stream, he started on a book about the animal, rewriting constantly as rejections arrived from editors and publishers: 'sordid', said one; 'too sad', declared another; 'people are not interested in the countryside', stated a third. The editor of *Pearson's Magazine* advised him *not* to keep on writing for the 'restricted animal story market'. Highly discouraging, for this was the world that interested him.

At this low moment, a two-acre field on the hill above Georgeham came on to the market. This was Ox's Cross, with 'a view over thousands of square miles of fields and valleys and sea and moor and estuary. And finest thing of all, a white owl lived in the wood, and flew around the field every evening as the sun was sinking down to the Atlantic to the West.'

Tarka the Otter had just been published after a final, triumphant surge of rewriting which lasted three weeks. A first edition of a hundred signed copies, printed on hand-made paper with hand-set type, would bring Henry a royalty of 40 per cent—£125 for the lot, or so he thought as he hurried to the owner of the field, offering that exact sum when he heard that someone else was bidding a hundred. The owner, who was the local butcher, accepted a cheque for twenty-five pounds as an advance, all that Henry's bank account contained. Then the prospectuses for *Tarka*, accompanied by encouraging letters, were sent out, and they waited for the deluge.

Nine people bought *Tarka* in the first week. By the end of a month, sixteen copies had been sold and the butcher was asking about the rest of the purchase money: 'The next morning a letter in a strange handwriting was brought up by Loetitia, with my early morning cup of tea . . . Immediately I was out of bed, and running downstairs in my pyjamas, told Loetitia that the otter book had won the Hawthornden Prize, which was £100 and fame! The field was safe!'

Tarka sold 3,000 copies the day after Williamson received the award in 1928, and has become one of the pleasures of growing up for generations ever since. It was hailed by Arnold Bennett as 'marvellous, and the writing of it is marvellous'. Henry may have his elfin moods, but never here. With the otter vulnerable to man and the elements, his lack of sentimentality is especially sympathetic to the young. It is a harsh book, tempered by such lyrical passages as Tarka's meeting with White Tip:

> He licked his face, while his joy grew to a powerful feeling, so that when she continued to disregard him, he whimpered and struck her with one of his pads. White Tip yikkered and bit him in the neck. Then she slid into the water and with a playful sweep of her rudder swam away from him. He followed and caught her, and they rolled in play; and to Tarka returned a feeling he had not felt since the early days in the hollow tree, when he was hungry and cold and needing his mother. He mewed like a cub to White Tip, but she ran away. He followed her into a meadow. It was strange play, it was miserable play, it was not play at all, for Tarka was an animal dispirited.

Henry Williamson's affinity with animals is unique. Apart from *Tarka*, he has written *Salar the Salmon, The Phasian Bird, The Gold Falcon, The Lone Swallows, The Peregrine's Saga,* and other wild tales, *The Old Stag*, and other hunting stories. But though he understands animals, there have been times when I wonder if he likes them, especially when I see Bonzo regarding him askance as he rubs her coat violently, the wrong way, exclaiming, 'Doggy, poggy, poor little man!'

I remember my disapproval as a boy when he took me otter-hunting, a sport he did not condemn at the time. Today he tends to hedge when he is pressed on the subject of hunting, and this is not speciousness. With his ache to remain objective, his views really are ambivalent, but 'The Badger Dig' conveys the way the bloodlust contaminated everyone taking part, including himself when he was blooded:

> I submitted; after all I was a guest. I was given a pad covered with short black hairs, with five digging claws, three of them broken, and I murmured thanks, and tried not to look unpleasant, as I wondered if the boar had broken them as he dug for the safety of his mate and himself. His labour availed nothing, for the pick and spade and harrying terriers working along a tunnel are more speedy than ten claws scratching on hard stone and earth. Now he was a lump without head and paws, and his blood was on my brow and cheek. I felt I had been false to myself, and yet another thought told me such feelings flourished only in nervous weakness. Why worry? And yet, only ten claws.
>
> With the dried blood stiff on my temples I climbed the hill, cursing the satanic ways of men, yet knowing myself vile, for they had not known what they were doing, but I had betrayed an innocent; and all the tears—weak, whisky tears—would not bring that badger back to life again.

This is one of the splendid stories in *Tales of a Devon Village*. Sadly, this book and the companion *Life in a Devon Village* are out of print.

The village, of course is Georgeham. After buying Ox's Cross on the hill above, he planted trees—fir, pine and beech—to form the vital windbreaks. In one corner he built, with the help of two friends, a small wooden hut where his children would be laid out to sleep on the floor after special outings, such as the jubilee of King George V when they saw the bonfires burning in celebration on the surrounding hilltops. For the family had grown too numerous to stay there permanently and they moved instead from the cottage in Georgeham to a fine, low, thatched house known as Shallowford, on the way to Taunton, and after that to a farm in Norfolk.

At the end of the war, his first marriage finished, Henry returned to Devon and the simple hut at Ox's Cross. He had been interned for a fortnight during the war, under the regulation known as 18B, because of his open support for Sir Oswald Mosley. To Henry's credit it is a loyalty that has been totally consistent but it has lost him the honour, a knighthood or the Order of Merit, that must have been his otherwise. His controversial beliefs stemmed directly from that First World War, the memories of which are stuck in his mind like the grooves of a gramophone record, sixty years later.

He is unable to escape, yet he can speak of this period with a strange affection: 'It wasn't such a bad war, really. I think we liked the Germans more than the French, they were our own stock.' His participation in the Christmas truce, when the two sides laid down their arms, convinced him of the futility of another battle with the Germans. He says of Mosley: 'He tried to stop the war with Hitler because he thought it would be the end of Europe. He was no traitor, he was a brilliant person.' As for Hitler, whom he met at the Nuremburg Rallies, 'Of course he was a great man, but so many great men turn out to be fiends and devils because they go too far. He wanted to avoid war with us, but he went the very way to get it. He was a very brave soldier and he loved England. He said there must never be war with England, if so everything would come to an end. There were tears in his eyes. He was a very emotional man.'

Henry's voice would be soft with admiration as he talked to me about Hitler when I was a boy. And I, who thought that Hitler was the very devil, was reduced to tears of impotent rage. Henry's sincerity made it all the more unbearable.

Today I am less passionate and can see the other side. I am not sure if this is a good thing, but I do believe that Henry's views, with their beginnings in the battlefield of the Somme, should be respected. Yet, even after all these years, there is suspicion of him locally because he has lived against the grain of his time. I have been assured that Henry covered his field at Ox's Cross with white lime in the war in order to direct the German bombers on their way to the RAF base at Chivenor. Apart from the fact that Henry was in Norfolk at the time, a more hopeless method of detecting an airfield in North Devon could hardly be imagined. Yet such stories have been repeated to me solemnly, as gospel. Though they would hate to think so, Devonians are great gossips. Henry has retaliated with bitterness: 'That's the sort of rubbishing thing you would hear . . . I don't care about people like that, they make me ill.'

It was such gossip that led to his internment, and the warning of the Chief Constable of Norfolk to stay indoors at night—'There are armed patrols who would be only too glad to shoot first and ask questions afterwards.'

Henry commented, 'How very funny, to have come to this.'

If Henry's views were occasional torment to me as a boy, I was a constant trial to him as I grew up. First I badgered him to write for the magazine I started at Cambridge, which he did graciously with an article 'My Friends the Crows'. I took a photograph to go with it, of Henry perched on top of the signpost at Ox's Cross, and sold a portrait to his publisher, which distressed him. He wrote forlornly as if I had 'taken' his portrait by stealth: 'So you have sold my ugly face to Faber. Will he stick pins in it: *I hate my face. It is ruinous and charred with sin.* O, the times one has thought of dissolution and peace in the tide surging north past the Morte . . .'

Next I committed the unforgivable intrusion of asking him to sign one of his books, unaware of his aversion to this practice and the way his earlier generosity had been abused. Characteristically, he sent me a long hand-written letter of explanation:

This may sound pompous and conceited; but in my small way and scope, in my own little life and sphere, it is how I feel. When one is asked to write in books, it is always a little offsetting: it isn't a spontaneous thing; writers know this feeling, and perhaps in the trade as it were, seldom ask one another to do it. It is in a way like love: it has to be the genuine thing, or it is no good at all, and should be avoided. Or it is like having a trout stream: the knowledgeable do not ask to be invited; they would not have the hands for throwing a fly exactly so, if they did. What does one do when a man turns up, complete with rod, etc., and says, 'You don't mind if I have a day on your

water, do you?' One used to say, 'Yes, but may I send you a
line first, next time, so that I can be sure of the water being
free for you?' But some of them, in the old Shallowford days,
did not understand that way of talking. They thought perhaps the owner was rude. No doubt he appeared so; but he
had so many requests like that, and each caller was unique to
himself, and did not know that he was but one of many. Of
course they were unknowledgeable; as we are all, until we
learn. So please Dan, try and see the question of the avoid-
ance of signing books by direct request . . . I have always
hoped that one day we might become real friends, so that I
will be able to give of my own free will. That's about the only
freedom left to one who has many responsibilities whatever
superficial adjudging might indicate.

That should have satisfied even me.

I find it hard to convey Henry's personality and do him justice.
Possibly because his very impartiality makes it difficult to grasp
him, but there is no doubt of one quality that he possesses to an
extent rare today. Few writers have devoted themselves to their
work as he has; constant rewriting, and anxiety always that he
has failed to reach the standard he has set himself. Three ver-
sions of *Tarka*, and he is still not sure which is the best, written
through the night, regardless of time. Was he happy in his work?
'It is true I may have suffered at the beginning, but when I came
into my style it was glorious. I was happy.'

When he completed the chapter on Maddison's death, 'I just
was in tears; I finished about eleven o'clock at night, I wandered
about outside, almost muttering "Willie's dead!" Not tears of
remorse; a feeling I had done something, achieved something, because there is no brutality or any unkindness in the writing, at
all.'

Altogether he has written more than forty books. The titles of
early works are evocative: *The Beautiful Years; Dandelion
Days; The Dream of Fair Women*. It is an honourable roll call.

His most ambitious work has been *A Chronicle of Ancient
Sunlight*, sixteen volumes started in 1951 and finished eighteen
years later. John Middleton Murry predicted: 'This will be in its
entirety one of the most remarkable English novels of our time',
but it has to be conceded that the formidable account of Willie's
successor, Philip Maddison, which echoes many of Henry's own

experiences, has yet to attain the popularity the nature books enjoyed. Perhaps it will happen, for booksellers are advertising for copies. Though Henry may be out of favour with the critics, few contemporary British authors command such loyalty from their public. When I wrote in celebration of his eightieth birthday in *The Daily Telegraph Magazine*, I was astonished to receive nearly fifty letters expressing appreciation and admiration of Henry Williamson's work. I cannot think of another writer who would inspire such a response.

In 1975 Henry visited the Grey House weekly, often daily. He looked magnificent as vigorously he drove his vintage MG with angry concentration down the lanes. But he tended to be absent minded, liable to arrive with an unexpected 'Sorry, I'm late', and leave with, 'All right if I drop in to see you, some time?' as if we had bumped into each other after several years. One sweltering day he arrived breathlessly on foot and exclaimed 'God! I hope you've got the wood for the coffin.'

He admits to loneliness with no animals of his own, though he has the affection of his son's gentle Alsation dog, Tree. Harry Williamson is in his twenties, a gifted musician and engineer, and the son of Henry's second marriage. He lives intermittently at Ox's Cross in a caravan. It is an odd settlement: a studio, the caravan, a large removal van painted in psychedelic patterns, the friendly wooden hut where Henry has written so much—though he has lost the will to do so any more. And, dwarfing all of these, the tall new house which rises on the summit above the trees he planted more than fifty years ago.

There is something Ibsenish about this building, which can be seen from miles around, even from the Taw and Torridge Estuary. Henry has never lived there, dividing his time between the wooden hut and his house in Ilfracombe, surviving on a diet of Cornish pasties and pub snacks, which make him feel rather wan—'I've gone down ten pounds recently.' Will Henry ever live in the tall new house that has cost him £27,000, 'the end of my cash'? This seems uncertain: the house is held in trust and intended for the various members of his families, to be used in rotation. He says he has loved three women in his lifetime, and thinks he has eight children. He told me wistfully, years ago, that he had been searching all his life for the perfect companion: 'And one day I shall die and go to my grave, and feel a salt tear on my coffin—"plop"—and up I'll jump, and there she'll be, too late.'

Recently, he confided his private hope that the house might become the Henry Williamson Museum, with his first editions and papers, his letters from Bernard Shaw and T.E. Lawrence, who had sent Henry a telegram shortly before he crashed on his motor-bike. There the house stands, waiting to honour the man who has received such meagre recognition in his lifetime. He was eighty on 1 December 1975.

In *Cakes and Ale*, Somerset Maugham described the reception accorded to Edward Driffield on his eightieth birthday:

> . . . it was a thoroughly representative gathering—science, politics, business, art, the world; I think you'd have to go a long way to find gathered together such a collection of distinguished people as got out from that train at Blackstable. It was awfully moving when the P.M. presented the old man with the Order of Merit.

It has always been assumed that Driffield was based on Thomas Hardy, and there is an irony here, for one of Henry's proudest claims today is the compliment paid to him by Hardy, Galsworthy and Masefield—'the Order of Merit fellows', as he calls them—'Do not worry about whether you will survive or not, you have written more classics than anybody in England at this time. You deserve the O.M. as much as we do.'

Certainly, in *Tarka the Otter*, Henry has written a book that can lay claim to the title of 'classic'.

The best moment on *his* eightieth birthday was no deputation alighting from the train at Barnstaple, but a reunion with his sons at the Imperial Hotel there that evening. As I write, he is ill, resting in a nursing home in London.

Thinking of him now, looking out on Baggy Point, I remember the ennobled bird the peregrine falcon. A pair of them used to live there until the tiercel was poisoned deliberately in the last war, because he attacked the carrier pigeons used by the RAF as they flew over Baggy Point. Consequently, small sacs of strychnine were fixed to their rings. Henry told me how he saw the remaining falcon go berserk with grief, racing out of the sky at a hundred miles an hour to attack any other bird she saw.

Coincidentally, the peregrine falcon was the subject of the last article written by the late Kenneth Allsop. When Ken was a boy, Henry's writing made such an impression that he cycled all the way to Ox's Cross to meet the author. After Ken's early and lamented death, it was Henry's melancholy honour to read the funeral address. It is not surprising that both men felt such an affinity with the falcon, for both have soared above the rest of us. At the end of the piece, Ken decried man's treatment of the bird: 'We poison them, we shoot them, we steal their eggs and young. It is so wrong. We are the predators and killers, not those peregrines. For they and the few of their kind which survive live exalted lives, true to their nature, and we degrade and damage their world which is so beautiful and complex and balanced.'

In a similar way, Henry has deplored the passing of so much wildlife that he has witnessed in North Devon. At least, through his books, we shall be able to recall the best of it.

A favourite passage of mine is found in the slender anthology *As the Sun Shines*, in his preface to the American edition of the 'Village' books, written when he was thirty-five. These are the final paragraphs:

> When I said that I wished I had returned from the wilderness before I began *The Village Book*, I meant that as man and writer I would like to be as the sun, which divines the true or inner nature of living things. When the rain drifts grey and cold in winter, when the north-east wind dries the lanes and withers fields and gardens, when the frost racks earth and water in agony then it is not seemly to seek Truth; but when the sun shines, there is a Being which unlocks and discovers the spirit of man or beast. The sun is entirely truthful; the sun sees no shadows.
>
> It is possible, by a sun-like understanding, to discover among the crotchety and cantankerous, among the so-called cruel and vicious, the same person as oneself; the human being which has grown from a child to its present shape, and which in its heart still has the solar innocence of the child. To be like the sun is to see all things plain, and to draw all life to oneself.

Sadly, Henry was confined to the airlessness of London in the endless summer of 1976, which he would have relished in North

Devon in earlier years. But on one of his last visits in 1975, I again dared the unforgivable and asked him to sign my copy of *Tarka*. He did so sweetly:

> This book, gladly signed for Daniel Farson,
> literary gent of a breed like unto my own.
> At Vention, a sunny evening, sky bright, and,
> at last, it is Summer come again!

February

Far from sunlight, the weather on this coast has turned to freezing. The winter is obeying its instinct, and I am delighted.

Unlike Henry, I welcome the rain-drifts, the cold and frost. This is a natural process. It was the continuing mildness, failing to crack the ground, that started to alarm me. I regard the present change as a penalty before the spring. It is not hard to endure; this is the perfect time of year to concentrate on work indoors, with no distractions outside, apart from the brusque, buttoned-up venture with the dogs.

I wonder if the chickens realise it will not stay like this forever. They are being 'hardened' with a vengeance. At first they were subject to the icy blasts of a bitter north-east wind, so tenacious that it rattled the windows. Now the wind has lessened, but it is so cold that their pan of water was frozen *inside* their hut when I let them out this morning. They are touchingly pleased to see me as they tiptoe into the great outdoors. It turns out that their beaks were deliberately broken to prevent them pecking each other; I thought this might prevent them from picking their grain, but they seem to have no difficulty, and no fear of me. Do they recognise me as a saviour? How maudlin can I get over a hen? Very maudlin, it seems.

When we go for our walk this afternoon, the wind has died completely and there is a faint fall of snow. The stillness is extraordinarily beautiful. A dog-fox with a white-tipped tail runs for cover against the skyline, and down the ravine beside the dense gorse that was burnt last year. There are flocks of birds everywhere; I shall try to identify them when I return home and remember, with shame, Ken Allsop's surprise on his last visit when I mistook a sparrow-hawk for something else: 'How can you live here, and *not* know?' he exclaimed. My ignorance is still abominable. And my large *Book of British Birds* has vanished. A guest? Probably, for people steal books with impunity as if it were not really stealing at all.

On my return there is one of the birds I've seen, unmistakable, in my *Countryside Companion*: the plover, with its tuft of a crest and white feathers underneath: 'Also known as the pewit', which explains the plaintive cry we have been hearing all day as if a small animal were hurt. If further confirmation were needed, the plover, pewit or lapwing is described as 'a member of a great flock over the arable ground in winter', and this has been true today.

I am certain that I also saw curlew, like large snipe, which I *can* recognise. The book informs me that the curlew 'flocks to the coastal mud flats in winter to feed on titbits left by the ebbing tide'.

I cannot understand why people talk of the deadness of winter. I find it vibrant.

chapter seven

The power of Lundy Island

I sat down opposite Shutter Rock, and took it all in, and yesterday I wrote it all out. When I got home I said to my wife,
'My trip, my dear, has cost me half-a-guinea, but I have put
five-and-twenty pounds in my pocket, for I have got a whole
chapter for *Westward Ho!*'

Charles Kingsley, on a visit to Lundy Island.

There is a thunderous climax to *Westward Ho!* as a ship of the
Spanish Armada is driven into the Bristol Channel, pursued by
the *Vengeance*:

'The dog has it now. There he goes,' said Cary.
'Right before the wind. He has no liking for us.'
'He is running into the jaws of destruction,' said Yeo. 'An
hour more will send him either right up the Channel, or
smack on shore somewhere.'
'There! he has put his helm down. I wonder if he sees land?'
'He is like a March hare beat out of his country,' said Cary,
'and don't know whither to run next.'

After two hours, with the *Vengeance* gaining rapidly in spite of the poor visibility, Salvation Yeo cries out the warning:

'Land right ahead! Port your helm, sir! For the love of God, port your helm!' Amyas, with the strength of a bull, jammed the helm down, while Yeo shouted to the men below. She swung round. The masts bent like whips; crack went the foresail like a cannon. What matter? Within two hundred yards of them was the Spaniard; in front of her, and above her, a huge dark bank rose through the dense hail, and mingled with the clouds; and at its foot, plainer every moment, pillars and spouts of leaping foam.

'What is it, Morte? Hartland?'

It might be anything for thirty miles.

'Lundy!' said Yeo. 'The south end! I see the head of the Shutter in the breakers! Hard a-port yet, and get her close-hauled as you can, and the Lord may have mercy on us still! Look at the Spaniard!'

Yes, look at the Spaniard!

On their left hand, as they broached-to, the wall of granite sloped down from the clouds towards an isolated peak of rock, some two hundred feet in height. Then a hundred yards of roaring breaker upon a sunken shelf, across which the race of the tide poured like a cataract; then, amid a column of salt smoke, the Shutter, like a huge black fang, rose waiting for its prey; and between the Shutter and the land, the great galleon loomed dimly through the storm.

He, too, had seen his danger, and tried to broach-to. But his clumsy mass refused to obey the helm; he struggled a moment, half hid in foam; fell away again, and rushed upon his doom.

'Lost! lost! lost!' cried Amyas madly, and throwing up his hands, let go the tiller. Yeo caught it just in time.

'Sir! sir! What are you at? We shall clear the rock yet.'

'Yes!' shouted Amyas in his frenzy; 'but he will not!'

Another minute. The galleon gave a sudden jar and stopped. Then one long heave and bound, as if to free herself. And then her bows lighted clean upon the Shutter.

An awful silence fell on every English soul. They heard not the roaring of wind and surge; they saw not the blinding flashes of the lightning: but they heard one long ear-piercing wail to every saint in heaven rise from five hundred human throats; they saw the mighty ship heel over from the wind, and sweep headlong down the cataract of the race, plunging her yards into the foam, and showing her whole black side

even to her keel, till she rolled clean over, and vanished for
ever and ever.

'Shame!' cried Amyas, hurling his sword far into the sea,
'to lose my right, my right! when it was in my very grasp.
Unmerciful!'

A crack which rent the sky, and made the granite ring and
quiver; a bright world of flame, and then a blank of utter
darkness, against which stood out, glowing red-hot, every
mast and sail, and rock, and Salvation Yeo as he stood just in
front of Amyas, the tiller in his hand. All red-hot, trans-
figured into fire; and behind, the black, black night.

Pedants are pleased to point out a slight inaccuracy in the
placing of the great Shutter Rock that caused the galleon to run
ashore. But the shipwreck on the jagged point of Lundy is wholly
credible when you stand on those cliffs yourself. For centuries,
the Bristol Channel was one of the great thoroughfares of the
world—'A million vessels, it has been computed, pass Lundy
Island every year,' wrote Warden Page in 1895. Lundy was the
solitary hazard. There was such a wreck as Kingsley described,
and it seems only right in such surroundings that the ship
should be described as 'He', appropriately for a man-of-war.
Charles Kingsley took the name of Cary from the former owners
of Clovelly, and the original Salvation Yeo is supposed to have
lived in a small cottage by the pier, now part of the Red Lion
Hotel. Yeo is still a popular West Country name. This tremendous passage, culminating with the flash of lightning that
blinded Sir Amyas Leigh and struck Salvation Yeo dead, conveys power and the past—the two outstanding features of
Lundy Island.

I look out on Lundy every day. The view from my bedroom
window would be incomplete without the island on the horizon,
a perfectly placed interruption on a line that might otherwise
become monotonous. And I have noticed a curious trick of perspective, that Lundy always looks as if it is exactly opposite even
if you are further south, at Clovelly, or north at Ilfracombe.

At night the lights blink their warnings from either end. The
name of Lundy is brought constantly to mind by the weather
forecasts: 'Lundy gale force eight, increasing locally, force ten.' I
rejoice when I see Lundy floating mysteriously above a line of
mist, for I know a heatwave is on the way and Lundy will disap-

pear for a week or more in the hot haze. There is a local saying:
'Lundy plain—the weather be rain, Lundy high—the weather
be dry.' It is true. That mist can also come in winter, and is mentioned in a verse called *Crossing* from *The Coasts of Devon and
Lundy Island* by John Lloyd Warden Page.

> I lay afloat in an idle boat,
> A fisher lad held the oar,
> Off a Devon strand, and watched the grand
> Old sea run up the shore.
> Old Lunday lay some leagues away,
> Guarding the middle sea;
> A silver mist his low length kissed,
> Yet rugged and cold looked he.

A few mornings ago, I drew the curtain and Lundy stood out
so vividly that I could see the lighthouses and cliffs and the
church on top. Today, in this white winter haze, Lundy has gone
completely.

The distance from the beach below me to Lundy is nearly
twenty miles. The island is three miles long and two miles wide,
surrounded by rocks with the evocative names of birds on the
eastern coast—Gull Rock, Gannets Bay, Puffin Slope, Kitti-
wake Gully and a more prosaic group known as the Hen and
Chickens. On the fiercer, western side, the names are appropriately harsher—Devil's Slide, Devil's Chimney, Jenny's Cove,
after the African trader that sank there loaded with ivory and
gold; and the Devil's Limekiln, next to the Great and Little Shutter Rocks at the point.

Some species of animal life have been introduced, like the delicate Japanese sika deer brought by Martin Harman in 1927, and
grey Atlantic seals can be watched from above. The indigenous
animals are hardly romantic: the pygmy shrew, only two inches
long, and the black rat.

It is the birdlife that is, or was, so remarkable. Lundy takes its
name from the Scandinavian words for puffin—*lund*, and
island—*ey*. Few birds are such fun to look at, resembling tipsy
judges with their red beaks and quizzical expressions. Irresistibly
comic yet tragically vulnerable, with their habit of laying their
solitary egg on the ground. Where there used to be thousands,
they can now be counted in hundreds or less. Walking along my

beach one warm spring evening after a storm, I saw a baby puffin, the beak pink rather than scarlet, washed up in the high tide, tossed about in the surf. When I tried to rescue it, the alarmed bird splashed away and I decided it was kinder to leave it to struggle to the land where it could rest. When I looked the next day, there was no sign of the exhausted bird so perhaps it survived and flew off to Lundy. In retrospect, I wish I had tried to save it.

Lundy has been famous for the birds that stopped there— pastor and hoopoe (I mention these for the ornithologist, not having the faintest idea what they are); peregrine falcon and chough; with such impressive visitors as the osprey and golden falcon, even an American robin which flew to Lundy non-stop, a distance of 3,000 miles.

When the blinded Amyas is led by Will Cary to the crag above the Devil's Limekiln, Kingsley refers to the birds disturbed by their approach:

> . . . a raven, who sat upon the topmost stone, black against the bright blue sky, flapped lazily away, and sank down the abysses of the cliff, as if he scented the corpses underneath the surge. Below them from the Gull Rock rose a thousand birds, and filled the air with sound; the choughs cackled, the hacklets wailed, the great blackbacks laughed querulous defiance at the intruders, and a single falcon, with an angry bark, dashed out from beneath their feet, and hung poised high aloft, watching the sea-fowl which swung slowly round and round below.

Once the birds were dense—in numbers, I mean—and unafraid of man. Philip Henry Gosse described them: '. . . on the hillocks, and in the hollows between, sit the birds indifferent to our presence until within two or three yards of them; the air, too, is filled with them like a cloud; thousands and tens of thousands are flying round in a vast circle . . .' But man was denser, and bird life has diminished over the years. So-called 'sportsmen' share the blame: woodcock and game were shot, and even the oyster-catcher and the puffin—'as good as chicken'—were taken for food. Gannets' eggs were collected from their nests, and sea birds netted at random. In an alleged 'good season', as many as 20,000 sea birds would be plucked for the value of their feathers, largely used to decorate the hats of society ladies. Twenty-four puffins yielded a pound of feathers and earned one wretched shilling. No wonder the gannet grew alarmed and flew north to Grassholm at the start of this century to escape the massacre and the din of the modern fog-horns.

The great auk, which is supposed to have bred on Lundy, was unable to leave because it was seldom known to fly—how it arrived in the first place is not explained—and the last auk was found on the island in 1849. Now the species is as dead as the dodo.

It is a dismal tale. John Chanter recorded more than 170 varieties of birds on Lundy but came to the conclusion: 'Much wanton slaughter has been committed by visitors shooting them down, as they sit in rows, indiscriminately, old and young, for the mere pleasure of slaughter, and without the probability of obtaining them when shot. This system has led to a scarcity of late in some of the rarer varieties . . .' Now, even the common varieties are threatened with the menace of man-made pollution fouling the sea. It can only be hoped that the new ownership of Lundy will protect the remaining birds, on the land at least, for the pleasure of watching them rather than the 'mere pleasure' of their slaughter.

The most curious feature on Lundy is the absence of the one thing you would expect—a jetty. It is hard to land and as hard to leave; infuriating to travel there on a Campbell steamer on a clear, calm day and hear a loudspeaker announcement at the last moment (following a radio disagreement between shore and ship) that there will be no landing after all. A trip round the sombre cliffs of the island and a refund of a fraction of your money is feeble compensation.

When you are able or allowed to land, the ship anchors offshore in the natural harbour and you are decanted into small boats, which row you up to the shingle beach. Then a stiff climb up the steep road to the cluster of buildings at the top, with a welcome pause at the Marisco Tavern. As Lundy knows no licensing laws, many visitors venture no further. Regrettably, the simple old hotel, where you read by candlelight at midnight and they bring you a jug of hot water in the morning, is temporarily closed.

Brian Waters, author of *The Bristol Channel,* has written that he first came to Lundy 'on a day of Mediterranean beauty' and Kingsley continued his description of the sea birds with the exclamation: 'It was a glorious sight, upon a glorious day. To the northward the glens rushed down toward the cliff, crowned with grey crags and carpeted with purple heather and green fern; and from their feet stretched away to the westward sapphire rollers of the vast Atlantic, crowned with a thousand crests of flying foam.'

Mediterranean? Sapphire? I have been to Lundy several times, but found it less exotic. I realise such colours do flourish—the postcards prove it—but cannot remember them so vividly. Brian Waters comments, 'One usually comes to an island expecting more and finding less than is to be found on the mainland.' Illogical, but true. I should have been more surprised if there were not such a resemblance to Baggy Point, so familiar already; certainly I should have been more excited if I had known the history of Lundy Island, which is bizarre.

The early years are predictable, apart from the discovery of tombs that revealed gigantic skeletons covered with limpet shells. One skeleton, perfectly intact, was measured before it was removed and found to be 8ft 2ins. long. Seven other skeletons were found and a mass of bones, as if bodies had been thrown into a communal grave. Also, bits of red pottery and beads of opaque, light-blue stone.

As the remains of women and children were found, it does not seem to be the burial ground after battle though it may represent the annihilation of an entire population. It has been suggested that the giants' graves were those of the Danes who fought the Earl of Devon near Appledore in 894. Their Raven, or Reafen, standard was seized and 1,200 men were killed, including their leader, Hubba. A stone at Bloody Corner records the battle:

> Stop, Stranger, Stop
> Near this spot lies buried
> King Hubba the Dane
> Who was slain by
> King Alfred the Great
> In a bloody retreat.

It was placed there by a Victorian historian, and can be found on

the road between Northam and Appledore. It is far from certain
that the information it proclaims is true; many places claim to be
the sites of Danish landings. But there is enough local reference
to make one wonder: the Hubba Stone, where Hubba was originally buried, cannot be traced, but a dockyard is known as Hub-
bastone Yard and a road up the hill from Appledore quay is
known as Odun Road, after the Earl of Devon. Then there is
Crow Point, on the opposite side of the estuary, supposedly
named after the Raven flag.

As for Lundy, the Danes had a custom of removing their dead
to a faraway place and the island would have made a natural
retreat for Hubba's fleet of twenty-three ships. This can only be
speculation, and there is no mention in the reports of the time
that any of the Danes was a giant.

Because of the difficulty of landing, and the security of the
high cliffs once they were climbed, Lundy was virtually impreg-
nable. It was therefore the ideal refuge for pirates. Piracy is such
a childhood image—peg-legs and parrots—that it is hard to see
Lundy as a pirates' lair, but this is exactly what it was.

First it was held by the Marisco family, who built their castle
in the twelfth century; the remains of it can be seen today. It was
a real fortress once, with walls nine feet thick. Chanter describes
the island then as a stronghold 'from which piratical attacks
were made not only on the high seas, but on the adjoining coasts,
the noble family of Marisco having degenerated into pirates, in a
chronic state of rebellion against the crown, and taking the lead
in all deeds of violence, but with varying success'. William de
Marisco brought matters to the boil when he hired an assassin to
murder King Henry III. The man was caught and in his con-
fession named William, who was denounced as 'having attached
to himself many outlaws and malefactors' while 'pursuing a
course of rapine and treachery'. Orders were issued to seize him
and William came to an unlovely end at the Tower of London;
his body suspended on a hook, lowered when stiff, disembowel-
led, and his entrails burnt. What was left was quartered and sent
to the four leading cities in the kingdom as a warning. His sixteen
accomplices were dragged by horses through the streets of
London before being strung up on the gallows, and Lundy
reverted to the King—briefly.

A number of barons were appointed governors—such as the Baron of Barnstaple, who was Lord of Lundy in 1245—until Edward II gave the island to his favourite, Hugh le Despenser. When Edward was forced to abdicate, he tried to reach Lundy but winds swept him north to Wales.

Considering how recent it is, the history of Lundy in the seventeenth century is astonishing:

1608   After complaints were made to James I, a commission sat at Barnstaple to hear of the merchants 'daily robbed at sea by pirates who took refuge at Lundy'.

1618   Sir Lewis Stukely fled to Lundy after betraying Sir Walter Raleigh who was attempting to escape to France. Around this time, a Captain Salkeld occupied the island and proclaimed himself King, even preparing for a coronation until his pirates resented such conceit and rebelled.

1625   Three Turkish ships landed at Lundy and occupied it for a fortnight, threatening to burn Ilfracombe. This confirms how valuable the position was to foreigners; otherwise it would seem a bleak destination after such a journey.

1632   The self-styled Admiral Nutt made Lundy his headquarters, in order to raid passing ships. A man-of-war was sent to capture him, but he escaped.

1633   A Spanish ship landed eighty men, who pillaged the island. A British naval captain complained to the Lord Treasurer: 'Egypt was never more infested with caterpillars than the channel with Biscayers.'

1634   Landing by a French pirate, Captain Pironville.

1647   Charles I appointed Thomas Bushell, who owned some silver mines at Combe Martin, as the new governor and ordered him to fortify the island against foreigners. When Charles fell, Bushell had to surrender the island to Richard Fiennes, who arrived at the Clovelly quayside with his soldiers.

1667   Gradually Lundy reverted to piracy, particularly vulnerable to attacks by the French, and the officer in charge of the North Devon coast issued a warning to the

Admiralty: 'Lundy Island is very slenderly guarded, four or five men from a vessel riding on a cross wind, crept over the gates and went to the people's houses before they saw anybody. If the Dutch should take the island it would block up the Severn, and a dozen good men could secure it from the world. Every Englishman should be instrumental to the security of his nation.' Sure enough, this prophecy came true a few years later when a ship flying the Dutch colours was driven in for refuge in bad weather. A boat was sent ashore with a request for milk for the captain who was sick, and this was supplied generously for several days by the residents who remained remarkably naïve in spite of experience. Finally the crew came ashore to say the captain was dead and asked if they could bury him in consecrated ground, which the islanders again provided readily, even agreeing to leave the chapel during the funeral service. The moment the doors were closed, the coffin was wrenched open, guns and ammunition handed round, and the crew, who were really the dreaded French and not Dutch at all, charged out to capture the trusting islanders. With no need to hurry, the French stripped the island bare—50 horses, 300 goats, 500 sheep, even the clothes off the backs of their prisoners—'and then, satiated with plunder and mischief, they threw the [islanders'] guns over the cliffs, and left the island in a most destitute and disconsolate condition.'

It is an interesting story, even if the coffin filled with guns seems faintly familiar. The word 'disconsolate' is perfect for the existence of the islanders. What could have induced them to stay? Apart from piracy, it was hard to grow sufficient food: the few cultivated fields were overrun by rats and rabbits and battered by the winds. Ironically, even water was and still is short, for the rain clouds that sweep up the Channel seem to divide at the island, pouring down on this part of the coast while leaving the island dry. There were no taxes, but there was precious little to tax. And yet with the peculiar blessing of our climate, which must be the least monotonous in the world, I can imagine that all hardship would be forgotten on that first exuberant spring day, and that the islanders knew their happiness—catching the famed Lundy lobster, watching the great migrating flights of birds swirl in to pause on their winter passage to the mainland.

In the eighteenth century Lundy changed hands constantly. The most spectacular owner was a swashbuckling character called Thomas Benson, son of a wealthy family at Knapp House near Bideford. He maintained a façade of respectability, becoming the MP for Barnstaple in 1749, but two years earlier he had landed a contract to transport convicts out of the country to Virginia and other southern states in America. Benson knew better than to do that. He set sail and, presumably protected by poor visibility, landed the men on Lundy. By day they were set to work building walls, at night they were locked up inside Marisco Castle. Benson sounds a megalomaniac, insisting on his right to receive a full naval salute from any passing ship and not hesitating to fire if they failed to provide it. Eventually he tempted providence too far. A few convicts managed to seize a longboat and cross the treacherous currents to Hartland Point, where they told their story and disappeared. The Sheriff of Devon raided Lundy and seized quantities of loot and tobacco carefully hidden in caves carved out of the rock. For this, Benson was fined £5,000. When he was charged with dumping the convicts, he pleaded that he *had* taken them out of the country—'They were transported from England, no matter where it was, so long as they were out of the kingdom.' He was fined £7,872 and his estate near Bideford was impounded.

Now he insured a ship called the *Nightingale*, a brigantine of eighty tons, laden with valuable cargo and bound for the state of Maryland. Instead, the captain of the *Nightingale* landed the cargo on Lundy, where it was quickly hidden by Benson as the ship put out to sea again and was promptly burned and scuttled on 1 August 1752. The crew were saved by another ship in the plot, but one of the sailors talked too much, plied with drink by Benson's enemies. This time the captain was hung at execution dock and Benson escaped to Portugal, though he is supposed to have returned to North Devon some years later in heavy disguise.

The island changed hands again in 1775 when it was bought

by Sir John Borlase Warren from the Estate of Earl Gower for a modest £510.

Peace descended at last when the island was bought in 1836 by a clergyman with the apposite name of William Hudson Heaven: inevitably, Lundy became known as 'the Kingdom of Heaven'. For once someone cared about the place. The Heavens constructed the road to the top, a considerable engineering feat, and built their home Millcombe House in the only gentle part of the island, surrounding it with oak, ash and hydrangea. It is a fine, unpretentious house, used as the hotel today, grand in its simplicity. Curiously, although no prison labour was used, it reminds me of mansions I have seen in Tasmania built by convicts around the same period: thick stone walls and strong materials, presumably local granite from the mine works that opened in the 1860s. With a large number of men employed in the quarry, if only temporarily, it seems odd that no attempt was made to construct a pier, but his son, the Reverend Hudson Grosett Heaven, had higher thoughts: a church to the glory of God, capable of seating two hundred when a congregation of twenty would have been optimistic. And yet this landmark, which would be more suitable in the Midlands and which towers over the shop, the tavern and the hotel, lends the island its character where a landing stage might have spoilt it forever. Built on the site of the old chapel, where they brought the coffin filled with guns, it is still known as St Helena, redolent of another lonely island. It was finished in 1897.

Warden Page wrote that 'Mr Heaven is, in fact—or might be if he chose—almost as much an autocrat as the Czar. The island is his absolute property, and he owes fealty to none.' But when this autonomy was practised by Martin Coles Harman, who succeeded the Heavens in 1925, he charged into trouble. Calling himself the King of Lundy, he conducted his own defence in the High Court in 1930 when he was prosecuted for issuing his own coinage: puffins and half-puffins. Harman claimed that 'Lundy is a vest-pocket size, self-governing dominion', and that the Bideford Justices, who had brought the case, had no right to do so. The Attorney General, however, summed up against him: 'Lundy seems to be Utopia but I think it would be just as happy if they had pennies with King George's head on them, instead of puffins with Mr Harman's head on.'

Lundy now entered a tranquil period, even enjoying the luxury of an airline which opened in 1935 with a twin-engined monoplane capable of carrying five passengers on ten flights a day. Apart from mail, freight included sheep, live lobsters, barrels of beer and sacks of corn. The pilot grew so familiar with the island he was able to make an emergency landing at night. By day he came in low, levelling swiftly on the strip before the wind blew him back, while the islanders held on grimly until the passengers had climbed out. The plane was blown over several times but not a passengers or sheep was lost. The return flight cost 12/6d for the twenty-five miles from Barnstaple, cut to sixteen with a detour over Baggy.

Lundy and Atlantic Coast Air Lines were suspended during the War, and after it all such airlines were nationalised, and the pilot lost his license—such is progress. One of the last planes to land was a German Heinkel which crashed in 1941, the crew were disarmed by the wife of a lighthouse keeper who took them into custody.

Albion Harman, the elder son, was killed in Burma, receiving a posthumous V.C. Martin Harman built a memorial which stands there today but family plans lost their zest. In 1969, after his death, the Harman family were forced to sell and Lundy suddenly hit the headlines. Several appalling possibilities were presented. The most drastic proposal was to adopt it as an English Alcatraz for long-term prisoners. Jeremy Thorpe agreed this was ideal from the security point of view, but soul-destroying for the prisoner to be cut off so irrevocably. A leading councillor and publican at Ilfracombe, Charles Disney, an American with a pleasing likeness to W. C. Fields, saw Lundy in terms of bunny girls and casinos exempt from licensing laws. Air strips and holiday camps were planned until the cost was estimated, when the Devon businessmen withdrew hurriedly. Meanwhile, the public began to realise Lundy's unique attraction: oil slicks perhaps, but still those flights of migratory birds and seals and porpoises, even a pair of peregrine falcons reported to be breeding there again. I wrote at the time:

> In these days, the independence of Lundy has an almost sym-
> bolic significance: no phones, no cars, no taxes, no laws. But

like many a paradise, there are boring practical snags—like
the difficulty of actually landing. People and supplies arrive
in a small boat and are then rowed ashore and towed by a
tractor up a steep path. The difficulty of transporting animals, like the wild ponies, can be imagined. 'Pimple' Symons,
who has taken off 150 since the end of the war, had to put
them in slings and swim them out to the waiting boat where
they were hauled on board. Then they were lifted off by
crane at Bideford quay and taken to Barnstaple market.
Conversely, he took Welsh mountain sheep to Lundy for
breeding, and now there is a flock of 500. 'Whoever buys
should make a proper landing place,' said 'Pimple', 'but let's
hope they don't spoil it. It's a wonderful place, when you're in
Lundy, you're in another world.'

The phone rang constantly at the estate agent's office in Barnstaple, with enquiries from abroad as well as from the immediate
locality. 'It looks as if the final figure will be well over £100,000,'
I was told, 'but how does one really value such an odd place?'

Major Moore started a campaign—'Save Lundy for yourself.
It's wide open for the wrong kind of harsh, commercial exploi-
tation and this is the last chance we will have to save it. At the
moment, Lundy is a wildlife sanctuary in practice, but is not designated as such—the danger is that whoever buys can do what
he likes with it.'

In the end it was Jeremy Thorpe who came to the rescue,
enlisting the vital support of the businessman Jack Hayward,
who put up the money to buy the island, and John Smith of the
Landmark Trust who offered to maintain it for the National
Trust. The island could hardly have fallen into safer hands.
Nature enthusiasts may strut in shorts by day and sing folk-songs
in the pub at night, but Lundy has been saved for the rest of us
too. If you wish to rent a cottage or stay at Millcombe House, you
can telephone the island's agent, Ian Grainger, at 0271–73333,
and he will give the information you need.

On my last visit, flying by helicopter with Jeremy and Marion
Thorpe, we were greeted by John Smith who happened to be
staying there. The Landmark Trust, which has saved and restored places of unique interest all over the country, is virtually
his private charity. A man of innate modesty but acute vigilance,
he is anxious to keep Lundy 'a tranquil, solid and unaffected

place with a life of its own.

Today there is an average population of thirty and the residents pay taxes. The days when Lundy was described as 'a lair of wolves' are distant, but problems remain. When John Smith offered to maintain the island it was a generous gesture and a bold one too. I doubt if he realised the hideous expense involved. Hearing a rumour that the island's future was in jeopardy, I wrote to him in 1976 and he sent me this word of reassurance:

> The future of the island? Shipping is the real problem, especially in winter. Lundy is twenty-five miles from the nearest harbour, further than England is from France—and it is the Atlantic Ocean, not the English Channel with which we have to deal; moreover the island is pretty inaccessible once you get there. However, it is worth a great effort. Lundy does have a remarkable power to refresh the spirits of its visitors. It is one of those simple places where you can hear earth's voices as they are indeed—where you can slow down and consider what you are doing; and the more people who do that the better for all of us.
>
> The island is a dreadful headache for us, but so long as people are appreciative I expect we shall persevere with it.

Lundy is fortunate in such ownership. The island could easily have been abandoned, too costly for any private family to keep. Instead of being restored, the few houses might have become shells—the wind whistling through the ruins of St Helena and Millcombe. This has been the fate of the Blasket Islands off the west coast of Ireland. It is claimed that no land lies between Lundy and Cape Horn; similarly, the Blaskets have been called 'the last parish before America'.

Because the Blaskets represent a simple way of life that no longer exists, they have a poignant significance in their dereliction today—which is why I leave the West Country for the West of Ireland in the next few pages.

chapter eight

The happiest people in the world

I have loved the Blaskets more than any other islands since my first sight of them one rare, hot evening several years ago. All too often they are obscured by a white, wet mist but this time they stood out—black silhouettes basking on a silver sea. I know that is a cliché, but it is how they were.

The Blaskets are the far western point of Europe, and my companion told me of the remarkable people who lived there until the last islander was forced to leave in 1954. When we parted, he urged me to read *Twenty Years A-Growing*, Maurice O'Sullivan's account of his boyhood on the Great Blasket, and by the time I returned to North Devon I felt convinced that my father must have possessed a copy—the island life sounded everything he admired.

I thought I knew all the books in the house, but I found O'Sullivan's at last on the top, dark shelf under the stairs—a dusty, splendid first edition, translated from the Gaelic. Occasionally an author can take you to another world, shutting out the present, and O'Sullivan did this for me. His book is a surge of innocence before he grew up and life became muddy. When O'Sullivan left the Blaskets he joined the police force and died mysteriously, from drowning. But he left this classic of childhood, which E. M. Forster compared in his introduction to the freshness of the egg of a sea bird, 'lovely, perfect and laid this very morning'.

By now I was determined to find out more about the islands. Intuition told me that my father had been there though he had never mentioned it. I searched through albums of old press cuttings until I found the account of his visit, in yellowing newsprint. This was published in the *Chicago Daily News* in 1928, a year after O'Sullivan left the Great Blasket for the last time and heard his dog barking behind him: 'Out on the bank howling as she saw me departing from her. I crushed down the distress that was putting a cloud on my heart.'

My father crossed the three and a half miles to the Great Blasket to meet the king of the island, Patrick Kane, but he had left for the mainland to collect the post. This is how my father described the king's return:

> Then I saw some black canoes putting out . . . An hour passed and they were under our cliffs, and then a man came up the path. He was dressed in a 'swally-tail' blue coat and wore a flat black felt hat.
>
> 'The King,' said someone.
>
> He was a fine king! He had a grand face, broad and big, pale with red freckles and bright blue eyes. Or were they grey? Because it was his smile that held you most. He had lived on this tiny island all his life and so had his father before him; and yet, when he laughed, it was the laugh of a man who knew the world. He told me that when Lindbergh crossed Ireland he past overhead. He saw him!

I vowed to follow in my father's footsteps—the Blaskets were in my blood—and luck was with me. I set out for the Blaskets in 1970, to film a BBC *Omnibus* on the late Brendan Behan; he too had loved the islands.

The fishing boat sauntered out of Dingle in the morning, a bustling village with a long jetty and a quayside of coloured houses and pubs—or rather shops with bars—side by side: no nonsense of them being spaced apart. The journey takes one and a half hours, past Ventry Bay, Dunquin and Eagle Mountain—one of the grandest panoramas in the world, when you can see it. A cascade of mountains from Mount Brandon in the north runs to the sea like waves; hills that are almost alpine with an Irish flavour of vivid green and wild red banks of fuchsia; while to the south, on the other side of the peninsula, the mountains of the Macgillicuddy Reeks are just a smouldering blur—on the rare hot day—like a barren Turkish shore.

These waters have some of the best fishing in Europe but a sudden swell can cast a boat up and suck it down violently on to a rock concealed the moment before. Someone pointed to the spot where the *Santa Maria* of the Armada was dashed to pieces on a rock known as 'the auld one', where fishermen threw plugs of tobacco to appease 'him' as they sailed past.

Because it was so abundant, it was years before the islanders realised the value of the seafood surrounding them, but when they saw the fishermen of Dingle making big money they joined in. So did the French, sending their boats to buy the lobsters at ten shillings a dozen.

Like Lundy, the Great Blasket has no proper landing stage, so we anchored outside. It was calm enough to let our dinghy slip between the two fingers of rock where we jumped on to the roughly hewn quay, but sometimes the swell is so strong that two or three weeks go by before a landing is possible.

As we rowed in, I stared at the grey ruined shells of the houses above. Can ruins suggest happiness? Because of O'Sullivan's stories, these did to me.

People say that the Great Blasket is the top of a mountain sticking out of the sea, just as Lundy is supposed to be an extension of Baggy Point, but it did not seem like this at all. The scene was slightly unreal, pastoral, though too immense to be cloying. Grey ruins against green slopes, and fields of moss and wild flowers so soft that I walked across them barefoot. There are no rats and no snakes but sheep stared at me perplexed. Looking round, I realised there were rabbits everywhere, poised in surprise. They are so unafraid that people catch them with their bare hands.

Below these fields, eroded by the rabbit warrens, lies the White Strand—a strip of sandy beach. I watched the journey of a large seal across the bay and scrambled down to swim myself, to share the pale clear water, unaware that a shark's fin had just been spotted cutting through the surface.

The beach is quiet now except for the repetitious collapse of the sea on the white sand, but once it rang with action. Sheep were driven here for shearing and islanders collected the black seaweed for manure. Tomas O'Crohan, yet another fine writer who lived on this small island, recalled the day when a school of porpoises was driven ashore and 'everybody you saw was crimson with blood instead of being pale or swarthy. The islanders had no lack of pork for a year and a day after that.'

Above all the Strand was a scene of wreckage. When O'Crohan was a boy he was told of the great 'wheatship', no vestige of canvas left except for a rag on the forecmast, which was blown on to the Strand. The people said they had never seen a wilder day and all the crew were lost, but the sacks of wheat saved the islanders in the worst year of the famine—'If it hadn't been for her, not a soul would have survived on the island.' Wheat that had spilled from the sacks was washed in spring water to get rid of the salt and then dried in the sun. The islanders boiled it into a thick mash: 'I used to hear the old hag saying it to my mother, again and again, that she never lived better in her life than the time it lasted. It was said she chewed the cud like a cow.'

There is a startling claim that Lundy Island was noted for its wine, as if this were due to vineyards rather than wreckage. In the same way, the larders of the Blaskets were stocked with sudden treasures, like brass bolts and lumps of palm oil. O'Crohan remembered the shipwreck of the *Quebra*: 'The sea filled up with everything eye had ever seen and that we had never seen in this place. I often heard the old hag over the way saying that God himself sent that ship amongst the poor.' One substance was used as a dye until they realised they could drink it; this was their first experience of tea.

As well as O'Crohan (he wrote *The Islandman*), there is yet another Blasket writer, Peig Sayers, a famous Gaelic story-teller who recorded *An Old Woman's Reflections*. She was born in

Dunquin on the mainland, but married an islander and lived there the rest of her life; she died in 1958. 'I never met my husband till the day I married him, but it was a love-match till the day he died. And why shouldn't it, for he was a big fine man.'

Lundy sported the colourful individual Thomas Benson, but the Great Blasket is unique in producing these fine writers. Tomas O'Crohan wished 'to set down the character of the people about me so that some record of us might live after us, for the like of us will never be again'. He described the routine of island life, though nothing could be less routine judged by today's standards.

There was tragedy: O'Crohan's first son was killed at the age of eight when he fell over the cliff, and Peig Sayer's son Tom also fell on to the rocks. He was so battered when he was brought home that his body could not be shown publicly. Remembering how she had to mould the head back to a semblance of shape, she made the simple comment, 'It was difficult. Let everyone carry his cross.'

The islanders had the gift of contentment. O'Crohan described the calm days: 'You would be sitting here on a day of sun, and the water moving on the rocks and the trawlers from Dingle sailing the bay, and you would say to yourself that there was no place more beautiful in the world, east and west.'

After the hard winter, 'hemmed in like a flock of sheep in a pen, buffeted by storm and gale, without shade or shelter', Peig Sayers welcomes the first warmth when 'the sea is polished, and the boys are swimming down at the shore. The little fishes themselves are splashing on the top of the water and even the old people are sitting out here and there sunning themselves.'

O'Sullivan, whose entire book is a celebration of youth, recalls the simple pleasures of special days, like the time he and another boy were given a lift to the mainland to go to the Ventry races:

> In we leapt, joy in our hearts, the two of us seated in the stern, the happiest creatures on the earth of the world. When we were a little distance out from the quay I looked back at the village and saw the boys and girls walking down.
> 'Look Tomas, what good luck we had to leave the quay in time!'

Laughing, he gave me a pinch in the thigh. 'Musha, it's true. If we were on the quay now we'd never get away.'

The sea was like a pane of glass, a stream of ebbing tide out through the Sound to the north, guillemots, razor-bills and petrels on the water, the four men stripped to their shirts rowing hard.

Such adventures would embrace all the islanders, like the summer evening when a great shoal of mackerel swam towards them. While the men raced out with their nets, the women hurried to the cliffs screaming directions at their husbands below.

There was not an old woman in the village but was already there, sitting on her haunches looking out at the curraghs. The evening was very still. It was a fine sight to look towards the shore of Yellow Island at the shoals of mackerel and the curraghs running round on them like big black flies.

There was no understanding the old women now, who were foaming at the mouth with their roaring.

'Your soul to the devil,' cried one to her husband, 'throw the head of your net behind them!'

'Musha, you're my love forever, Dermod!' cried another when she saw her husband making a fine haul of fish. One woman, Kate O'Shea, her hair streaming in the wind like a mad woman's, was screaming: 'The devil take you, Tigue, draw in your nets and go west to the south of the Sound where you will get fish for the souls of the dead. Och, my pity to be married to you . . .'

Many thousand mackerel were caught that night.

When O'Sullivan was old enough to join the fishermen, he found it less romantic, as he told his grandfather on his first day: '"I think, daddo, there is nothing so bad as fishing."

"You may be sure of it, my bright love."'

O'Sullivan was making fun of his dissatisfaction, but he was one of many islanders who were losing that contentment with their simple life. One day he told his father he was leaving:

He looked into the fire thinking. At last he looked up: 'Are you in earnest?'

'I am indeed.'

'When will you be going?' said he with a sigh.

'Tomorrow.'

'Well, I give you my blessing, for so far as this place is concerned there is no doubt but it is gone to ruin.'

On my visit I could see the ruins, the prophecy of O'Sullivan's
father confirmed, but the island was inhabited again. Two men
were spending the summer in one of the derelict houses, a teacher
from Dublin and his uncle who was eighty-seven years old. The
old man had been born on the island, though he spent many of
his early years in America, and had reverted to his Gaelic tongue.
His nephew, who acted as interpreter, told me that this annual
return to his birthplace was the incentive that kept the old man
going. At first he was too shy to meet me, because of an unsightly
ear infection, but after a few words from his nephew I was allowed inside the bare stone house with whitewashed walls and
learnt about the king, and his role as spokesman and postman of
the island, and of the sheep and cattle carried from the mainland
in their slender curraghs. The idea of a cow in such a delicate
craft seems incredible—one kick would have shattered the fabric
of wooden slats and tarred canvas—but the feet of the animal
were bound and it was stretched upside-down on a bed of
bracken until it was comfortable, or too terrified to move.

The old man told me that after the First War there were 250
people on the island, 1,000 sheep, thirty cows and twenty-nine
horses, whose young stock were swum across the bay when the
weather was calm to be sold on the mainland. Eighty children
went to school and learnt enough to leave for America, sending
money back for the fares of their younger brothers and sisters;
occasionally to return, like this old man.

The island life had become too hard, in the minds of the
young. Admittedly, they were poor in one sense, the houses only
ten to twenty feet long and, in O'Crohan's case, so close together
that if 'the old hag' had wanted to 'she could have scalded my
mother from her own doorway with boiling water'. Apart from a
spinning-wheel, the only decorations were holy pictures and por-
traits of national heroes, or washed-up light bulbs used as orna-
ments. Much of the furniture was made from wrecks. A partition
divided the houses in two—on one side the beds, with sacks of
potatoes stored underneath and barrels of salt fish in the corner,

and on the other the kitchen where the family passed the day. They must have gasped for space at night, especially when they shared with a cow and a calf, an ass, two or three dogs and a pet lamb. If the grandparents were alive, they slept on the floor near the turf fire, puffing away at their clay pipes. In the niche beside the chimney there might have been a cat, and kittens, and a pot hanging above the hearth. The roofs were made of thatch and children scrambled on top to collect the eggs that the hens laid in the rush. Later the roofs were made of tarred felt, and the animals kept outside in a separate shed; no wonder the children welcomed the spring and football in the fields.

A stifling winter existence—to *us*—but they had the distraction of story-tellers, like Peig, and nightly dancing in the larger houses. There was a special house where boys and girls could stay until midnight, and O'Crohan assures us proudly, 'Nothing wrong ever happened among them for the sixty-seven years that I've known it.'

I found it moving that the old islander wished to return to the echoes of this simple life before he died. When I mentioned the two men, as we chugged back by boat to Dingle in the evening, I was asked, 'What can they find to *do*, with no pub or telly?' and I thought of them, revelling in their solitude. As for the Great Blasket, this was dismissed also—'If only there had been some sign that human beings had lived there, a scrap of faded wallpaper, I might have felt something. But the ruins were as impersonal as Pompeii.' I smiled again at the thought of wallpaper—Sanderson's perhaps?—in these rough homes, and remembered the atmosphere of the ruins of Pompeii when I saw them.

The Blaskets had me enthralled. There are six islands altogether, with Innish Tooshkert lying like a sleeping giant to the north, the face in profile, a slight paunch in the middle. Outwardly, there is much in common with Lundy. The Great Blasket is roughly the same size and there are signs that people lived there a thousand years ago as they did on Lundy. Some ancient race built a fort on the summit of the Blasket, then the Danes invaded, and a tower dating from the French wars stood intact until it was shattered by a thunderbolt. There is a curious parallel between the martello tower on the Blasket and the Marisco Towers on Lundy. According to Chanter, 'These are supposed to be of great antiquity, and from the descriptions which have been handed down, appear to have had many of the characteristics of the Irish round towers, in shape, size and position of the door-ways much above the ground level, which may be explained by the intimate associations of the earlier Marisco lords with Ire-land.' Sir Geoffrey de Marisco was appointed Lord Justiciary of Ireland in 1231.

Certainly the round towers were one common landmark on the two islands, but on my journey back to Dingle I was puzzled by the sense of something missing—eventually I realised it was the church, which dominates Lundy today.

I still find it curious that the Gaelic community did not build a church of some sort, though apparently there was a small grave-yard, now submerged, for children who were stillborn and for the decomposed bodies of sailors washed up by the sea.

When an islander died the body was taken to the mainland in a funeral cortège, as many as eighteen curraghs drifting across the bay. Burials and marriages were performed in the old church at Ballyferriter and were celebrated in the pub afterwards: 'There was no silent drinking then. Into the tavern and out of it without a word said.' Instead, O'Crohan wrote,

> There would be as many as twenty men in the room drink-ing, and every man that came in he would not go out without singing a song or telling a tale. And you would go down into the street, there would be noise coming out of another tavern and it would be the same there, tales-a-telling and songs-a-singing and no man quiet. There were four pubs in Ballyferri-ter, each with a fiddler of its own, and many of the guests ended the wedding night in hospital.

O'Crohan stressed that 'you would hear no word of English', and this is the greatest difference between Lundy and the Blas-kets, that in times of trouble the Great Blasket was a place of refuge, not for pirates, but for the Gaelic tradition. In this way the island fulfilled a purpose. Were the islanders a nobler people because of this? Or were they really the same as any villagers on the mainland? Anxious to learn more, I asked about the islanders in Tom Long's pub, back in Dingle that night. He told me that one of the survivors lived nearby, and took me to see him. Sean

Kearney had a brick-red complexion and gave a huge laugh at the end of every sentence, possibly because our conversation was so strange. We spoke in English, but our accents were so foreign to each other that Long's ten-year-old son had to act as interpreter.

Three Kearney brothers had sailed from Ventry and settled on the Blaskets four hundred years ago.

'Were the islanders really happier than most people?' I asked him.

'Happy? As happy as anyone in the world, just as the rabbits are today. Any place where you are born is all right, but we had dancing *every* night and playing cards, and visitors in the summer, English, German, Irish, all come to speak Gaelic.'

'Were there fights in such a small community?'

'Fights?' he looked surprised. 'Never. It was fishing and work all day and happy in the night, we never had the time. Everyone was busy keeping everyone else.'

'Why?' I asked, meaning it sounded too virtuous to be true.

'We *had* to.' He gave a thunderous laugh. 'We want you tomorrow, but you may want me the day after.'

Though never king, Sean's father had been the postman going to the mainland three times a week for a weekly salary of a pound. Sean was the last sub-postmaster in 1940, when there was a radio link.

'Why was there never a proper landing stage?' I asked.

'Bad government.'

'What did you eat on the island?'

'Potatoes, three times a day. Soup off the rabbits. No flour, no sugar, no tea. In old days we'd make our own butter and put it into a bog and keep it forever. My grandfather was ninety-nine years old; if you gave him a sweet cake he'd throw it between your two eyes.'

Fish was the main diet, after potatoes, especially boiled mackerel, which they salted down for the winter. I asked about the chickens who made their nests on the roofs. 'No good,' said Sean. 'I'd rather a sea bird, rather a puffin or a seagull if they're young. Boy, they're good! Rather a puffin than any steak.'

He told me he believed in fairies—though he might have been indulging in the well-meant Irish courtesy of telling the visitor what he wishes to hear. 'The old people heard them every night,' he said, 'singing and crying.'

'Was that unpleasant?'

'They were all right sometimes. They're not there now, there's too much traffic in the world, but they were there then'—and he gave another of his hearty hoots of laughter. 'When I was seventeen, I came back from fishing and saw a lady standing near the house and she was as white as snow, and out of her mouth a flame. "What's wrong with you?" asked my father. "Look," I said, "look, see that." Boy, he crossed himself, he always carried holy water and sprinkled it just in case. She disappeared and we went home and we were sweating. Sweating in bed I was, and we'd had no porter that day!'

I asked the crucial question: 'What was the difference between the islanders and those on the mainland?' He gave a delightful grin: 'We were like fish out there, oh so lively! On the mainland they were like snails.'

The next morning I drove to Ballyferriter in search of another islander, Tom Daly. After stopping at several houses, I found him and his brother with two affectionate, foolish sheepdogs in their garden, a tremendous sweep of fields behind them and the Blaskets vivid in the distance. Daly is the last craftsman to make the black curraghs or canoes—he calls them 'naovogs'—which are still rowed across from Dunquin to the island. Once they were built to hold a crew of eight, then four, and Daly's boats now seat three. It seemed unthinkable that such a framework could support anyone in winter storms, yet they have proved the strongest craft of all and Daly could not remember a single death by drowning though he was born on the Great Blasket in 1900. Their lightness made them easy to manoeuvre between the narrow shelves of rock, though they tied a bottle of holy water and a medal on the prow for good measure. Looking into Daly's workshop, I was surprised to find it bare except for a few basic tools—a grindstone, axe and plane. The rest of the equipment was his eye, his touch, his skill.

Back in the pub, Mrs Long told me of Tom Daly's father, who had been famous for the violins he made by hand: 'He was a lovely man. He had a culture and a kindness, something you don't find every day.'

I asked, again, if the islanders had been a special race.

'They were the happiest people in the world,' she said.

Mrs Long gave me the name of the last teacher on the Great Blasket—Mary Fitzgerald, now Mrs O'Brian—and I traced her the next evening in a small fishing village near Kenmare, on my way back to England. 'You're the first man who has spoken to me of the Blaskets since I left,' she exclaimed, as she let me in.

There were thirty-three pupils when she arrived in 1934; only nine when she left in 1940. By then they were more sophisticated than the children in O'Crohan's time, who screeched and roared with laughter when the School Inspector came over from the mainland, 'a man with four eyes'. He was the first man they had seen wearing spectacles.

Gaelic was forbidden on the mainland by the British then, and a child could be punished if caught reading a Gaelic book, but on the Blaskets it was English that was the difficult new subject.

Mrs O'Brian also remembered Tom Daly's father. 'A musical genius. Once he visited Innish Tooshkert, one of the other Blasket Islands, and thought he heard the fairies playing a tune which he memorised and played to the islanders afterwards. They called it the Fairy Tune, it was very sorrowful.'

'Did any of the islanders want to leave in '54?'

'Oh they did!' she said. 'You see, it was the old story of the young people wanting to improve themselves, they were more aware of the dangers of the life than the older generation of fishermen, and they didn't seem so skilled any more.'

This is the theme of the Blasket Islands—a loss of skill and spirit, the price of 'progress', the son lesser than the father. Before I left, I had gone to see O'Crohan's grave near Dunquin, dark and overgrown, with the Blaskets dominating the distance, as Lundy does in Devon. The simple epitaph gave the final word: 'The likes of us will not be there again.'

chapter nine

A perfect freshness

The hens have laid their first egg. Absurd excitement—or is it so absurd? A perfect freshness: an orange yolk, a white that holds its shape when poached. From now on, omelettes will have a new lustre.

An egg is an egg is an egg is not true. Anyone who thinks a battery egg is the same as a fresh one must be unable to tell margarine from butter, Smash from mash, or plastic-wrapped pulp from new-made bread.

It is the first day of March, so suddenly and gloriously hot that I open my balcony door for the first time this year. It is rusted from the sea-storms and I have to use oil and hammer. Sitting outside afterwards, I can feel the sun and see daffodils on the lawn below me. Winter is nearly over.

From my window on the sea I have been able to watch spring approaching. The sunsets have moved along Baggy Point towards the open sea. Any evening now, the sun will round the land and sink into the water. Then I shall know that spring has arrived. Spring: the most vital and yet the most lethal time of year, a period of suicide when people find the resurgence of life around them too cruel a contrast with the meanness of their own lives.

Spring is sheer hell to write about. Even the mention of the cuckoo is redolent of nursery whimsy, though I find its call the most reassuring sound of the year. Words fail me. The finest passage on spring that I have come across was typed out by my father, and is now tacked on the wall of my bedroom.

'I don't know how long ago it was when I first read these words,' wrote my father at the top of the page, 'in Tsarist Russia very likely; when, driven almost to a nervous breakdown by trying to get a straight answer from the Russian War Department, I took to reading the great Russian writers for consolation; and, if I could find it in books, some clue to the incredible be-medalled generals I had to deal with. These are the opening lines of Tolstoy's *Resurrection*, published in 1889:

> No matter that men in their hundreds of thousands disfigured the land on which they swarmed, paved the ground with stones so that no green thing could grow, filled the air with fumes of coal and gas, lopped back all the trees and drove away every animal and every bird: spring was still spring in the town. The sun shone warmly, the grass came to life again and showed its green wherever it was not scraped away, between the paving stones as well as on the lawns and boulevards; the birches, the wild cherries, and the poplars unfolded their sticky and fragrant leaves, the swelling buds were bursting on the lime trees; the jackdaws, the sparrows and the pigeons were happy and busy in their nests, and the flies, warmed by the sunshine, hummed gaily along the walls.
>
> Plants, birds, insects, and children rejoiced. But men, adult men, never ceased to cheat and harass their fellows and themselves. What men considered sacred and important was not the beauty of God's world given for the enjoyment of all creatures, not the beauty which inclines the heart to peace and love and concord. What men considered sacred and important were their own devices for wielding power over their fellow men.'

So it *is* possible to write about spring, with a magnificence I shall not attempt to emulate.

There has been a tremendous sea these last few days. Little wind, but lines of surf starting to form far out, sweeping in as high as houses.

The spray rises from the rock beyond Baggy Point; high tides have clawed at the foot of our wooden steps, eating the sand away. It has been invigorating to walk with the dogs, running to escape the sea as it surges in, jumping to safety on a newly formed sandbank, trapped briefly on some rocks, or caught by a sudden wave, which left the dogs startled and awash and myself soaked to the knees.

There have been especially low tides too. At midday I noticed a large black shape off Baggy Point. Looking through the binoculars, I thought I saw a fin, which led to instant speculation: shark, porpoise or whale? Or merely an immense log? Though it vanished, to reappear suddenly with a fountain of spray, it stayed in the same position. Swinging the glasses towards Morte on the other side of the bay, I saw the line of rocks more clearly exposed than ever before—it would have been possible to scramble along them to Morte Stone for this brief moment at least. Back towards the mysterious object: still there. And then it dawns on me: this is Wheeler's Stone. It is marked on all the maps but this is the first time I have seen it since I came here. The fin is revealed as a jagged rock snared with seaweed.

Until now I had assumed the maps had mistaken the position, confusing it with the rock we know as Polaris and marking it too close to the shore, but there it is exactly as indicated. I learn later that a sailor on the *Bessie Gould* jumped on the stone at another low tide and claimed it for Queen Victoria. His name was William, or Willer Luscombe, and it became known as Willer's Stone, altered further by the Ordnance men to Wheeler's Stone.

Now I wonder why there is no mention on their maps of the Polaris rock. Sailors who are unfamiliar with these waters might skirt the end of Baggy Point and aim for this very spot, which seems safe, only to strike it.

A large white goose stands surprised on the bare sands as the tide goes out. Could this be a snow goose? Yet again, I wish I knew more about birds. It looks as if it should be—a large bird of ten pounds or more, perfectly white apart from wing tips and a few tail feathers. It's different from the large grey Canada goose that circled overhead, as if it was searching desperately, while I had a final morning swim last November. It had stayed for two days and then flown off during the night.

There has also been a solitary white swan, resting on the water in the corner of the bay, looking curiously out of place in the open sea.

I make a foolish attempt to lure the white goose with a slice of bread—'Dear goose, stay with us and we shall look after you.' This offer is rejected by an indignant squawk as it flies out of reach. Now it sits, gigantic and disconsolate, among the gulls.

In spite of these tides, there has been little flotsam and jetsam, though I did find a yellow ball for Streaker who carries it proudly. Is flotsam the debris at high tide, and jetsam at low? The dictionary is little help, suggesting that flotsam is 'wreckage found floating' while jetsam is 'goods deliberately jettisoned from ships'. As both are bound to be washed ashore in the end, surely they must be the same?

When I came here first a quantity of wreckage was cast ashore, including a number of planks that I used to build the steps down to the sea, and a couple of garden benches. There were, too, those green glass balls used in fishing nets, which I see now in souvenir shops. The floats today are made of plastic, but so is everything—plastic or polystyrene—this is the wretched flotsam I find now. Occasionally thousands, possibly millions, of translucent beads, resembling pearls from a distance, line the edge of the tide. A closer look shows they are industrial waste washed across the Bristol Channel. They float under the surface and when some local mackerel were split open, several of these objects were found inside.

Plastic is the enemy because it does not rot: sheets of plastic, plastic dolls, plastic bottles. Worst of all is the plastic container with pretensions; I have come across one shaped as a Grecian urn. The tacky texture of the fake posing as the classic original was especially unpleasant.

I found a bottle once with a message inside. It came from a schoolboy in Bude who gave his address and asked for a reply. I was leaving on a Peace Cruise to the Baltic and took his note with me, thinking it would be fun to reply with a Russian stamp and appropriate name, *Danil Farsonovitch*, saying his bottle had just arrived at Leningrad. But the Peace Cruise proved far from peaceful due to my toasts on the anniversary of the Hungarian uprising, and I left the ship at Copenhagen. I forgot all about the bottle but I wish I had replied; even a message from Denmark might have startled him.

I have yet to find a full wine bottle, though I live in hope. I have been told of 'a close shave' several years ago, one Christmas Eve, when a Spanish cargo ship appeared to go berserk off Morte Point, careering in circles with no one visible on board, like a ghost ship. Villagers shouted their warnings against the wind, unaware that the cargo was wine and the crew were drunk below. Incredibly, it kept missing Morte Stone by inches until the captain came to his senses and struggled on deck, where he seized the wheel and straightened his ship towards Bristol. What beachcombing that would have been, on a Christmas morning too.

Recent, though more prosaic, finds have included a wooden trough. At least this has proved perfect for feeding the hens with their mash in the morning, just the right length and depth, and heavy enough not to tip over when they cluster along the edge.

And there is the snow goose. Since his or her arrival, I have come across this passage in *Sand County Almanac* by Aldo Leopold, an American who died in 1948 when he was sixty-one, helping to fight a fire on a neighbour's farm in Wisconsin. I liked the sound of him after reading the first sentence: 'There are some people who can live without wild things, and some who cannot.'

Leopold described the March geese that weaved down to his lake every spring. 'Once touching water, our newly arrived guests set up a honking and splashing that shakes the last thought of winter out of the brittle cattails. Our geese are home again!' He counted as many as 642 geese in 1946, noting the occasional lone goose among the great flights that stopped near his farm. He concluded 'that flocks of six, or multiples of six were far more frequent than chance alone would dictate. In other words, goose flocks are families, or aggregations of families, and lone geese in spring are probably just what our fond imaginings had first suggested. They are bereaved survivors of the winter's shooting, searching in vain for their kin.'

A paragraph in this morning's *Daily Telegraph* has supplied a further explanation: 'Whitefronted geese, which fly into Somerset from the Soviet Union every year, are gradually being driven away by watersports enthusiasts and drainage experts, the Somerset Trust for Nature Conservation stated yesterday in its annual report.' Perhaps one of those whitefronted geese has come here.

There is a possible postscript to the visit of the grey Canada goose last autumn. It is conceivable that the bird flew north to Lynton and mated with a more domestic goose called Sally, who had been known to local children for several years. Sally kept close to the river banks above the busy harbour, but a wild Canada goose joined her from time to time. He became known as Gregory.

This spring there were five eggs in the nest and local children watched hopefully, but in vain. For once, humanity is not to blame. Wild mink are breeding in the valley and a few nights ago a pair struck at the nest and savaged Sally to death as she defended it. Gregory arrived too late, but killed one of the mink at the end of a 'bloody battle', after which the second mink fled. Now Gregory guards the remains of the nest, his wings spread out protectively though there is nothing left to protect. A futile but noble gesture by the bird, whose mind must be a turmoil of grief.

Jack Boucher, along the road, tells me he has seen a dark blue mink in the scrub below Baggy. I did not pay all that much attention until now. If a mink can kill a goose, what a holocaust there would be if it got at our timid hens. They are locked up tonight with extra care.

In retrospect, the finest piece of flotsam on this shore was found by Peter a few years ago at high tide, half exposed in the surf. A darkish object, presumably driftwood, but such a curious shape that he went to investigate. He realised it was the bone of a large animal, two feet high and nearly three feet across on the sides which resembled wing tips, and so waterlogged he could hardly lift it.

Knowingly, I identified the bone as part of a cow that had

fallen off the cliffs. As it dried and whitened, Peter had it confirmed as the vertebra of a whale. If there were thirty of them it must have been a vast creature, but books from the London Library refer to whales the size of elephants. Certainly it could not have come from the small whale washed ashore at Croyde before the First World War, photographed with Tom Parsons's 'granfer' standing on top.

Was this washed ashore, or uncovered by these exceptional tides? It remains a mystery—polished by the sea and sand so the edges are smooth to the touch; as perfect as if it were machine-turned; as human as a figure by Henry Moore, complete with the hole for the spinal chord. Perhaps a comparison with Brancusi is better, for its form surges upwards with the elation of a bird. Yet it's so much finer than anything man-made. A ghostly presence, fierce but friendly, it looms whitely in the corner of the sitting-room, an essential part of the house.

More about dogs

Bonzo was born several months after Littlewood died, and would have been her great-granddaughter. Bassey is her grandmother and Alice her mother.

Bonzo is a constant joy, quite irrepressible—not that I wish to repress her. She was picked from the litter for the wrong reason: because she looked so comic. She has an alert little face that still makes people smile. Her ears grew in the wrong direction and perch up oddly even now. There are two or three white hairs at the furthest tip of her tail and she has white feet—slippers at the back, boots in the front. And a perfect white nose. From a distance this shines brightly, for her eyes disappear into the blackness of her coat—she is all nose.

Bonzo reacts to every noise and movement. People assume she is nervous; in fact she is hysterical. She screams with delight when she greets the others as they are let out of their kennel in the morning; she yells with ecstasy if we go for a walk; she shouts with relief when I return after an absence. I have never known a dog talk so much.

Of course there is no such thing as a comic dog, only a comic owner.

There are moments when Bonzo seems mystified by so much happiness. I can recognise these shades of character now, and when we are alone I praise her gravely in case she needs reassurance that she is not really a comic after all. At such moments she is calm, giving me sidelong looks, all white of eye.

I was startled when a boy exclaimed, 'That dog looks more like a cat!' and astonished when a friend made the hurtful remark: 'You could never call her a pretty dog, could you?' I looked at Bonzo. That delightful face smiled back. How odd that my friend should fail to see her beauty.

Her closest friend is Streaker—the dog that belongs to Frances. They play together endlessly, after their breakfast Bonio, racing down to the sands where they whirl and twirl in circles. Suddenly they stop, crouch—then off again, stalking each other through invisible 'high grass'.

All Streaker demands is to have a ball thrown for her. Then Bonzo waits further back, like an anxious goalie. She has no interest in the ball: her role is to seize Streaker by the neck as she runs after it. This must be part of their game—otherwise Streaker would find such a growling, cumbersome object too maddening to endure. And it must be loyalty that makes Bonzo so persistent, for she never enjoys the game herself. Her toy is an avocado pear stone, which she tosses into the air.

In the evenings, after the others are locked up, Bonzo and Streaker play on their sofa, emulating lions and tigers. They know how far to go, by a whisker: Streaker snapping her powerful teeth ferociously, Bonzo leaping out of reach. Then that sudden silence as they freeze—and off again.

They are complete opposites: Streaker large and amiable, Bonzo small and sharp. At times Bonzo's loyalty is alarming, for her size belies her strength. When Blacky was trying to intimidate Streaker, Bonzo tore into her with such ferocity that there has been no such bullying since.

On another occasion I was listening to the radio in the porch when a lady told Pete Murray that the correct way of praising a dog was to say 'What a good dog!' emphasising the *t* in the 'what'.

'WhaT-T good dogs!' I repeated. In seconds there was a furious dog fight with Bonzo pinning Blacky to the ground, her teeth embedded in the top of Blacky's head. My frantic attempts to separate them were useless. Luckily a container of water was nearby and I hurled this over them. When I led Blacky into my bedroom, our nerves were equally shattered though I suspect that Blacky's trembling was due more to injured dignity than to pain. Later I was astonished to see the two of them licking each other.

Less amusing was an incident last night. This concerned Pencil, the half-whippet who is Littlewood's daughter and the oldest of the dogs today. She is approaching the end of her days, but has the sense to save her energy, sleeping for hours until she emerges into the sunlight when she wriggles happily on her back.

Usually she eats on her own, but for some reason I let them all eat together last night. I heard the usual growls, but a protracted burst made me hurry down to find out what was happening. Pencil was standing there miserably, and I have the uneasy feeling that both Bonzo and Alice had attacked her. Though the back of her coat was wet there was no injury; her expression of dejection was bad enough. She slept as usual on the sofa in the sitting-room, but it was the sleep of exhaustion, not the usual dreams as she raced after rabbits in remembered youth, with legs twitching and faint moans of excitement.

Such bad temper is hard to forgive and Bonzo knows she is unpopular, yet this was only a moment of viciousness: she is not that way by nature. Indeed, her concern for Bassey has been touching.

Bassey is a game old dog. Her cheerful black-and-white face is scarred from plunging into brambles after rabbits; her eyes water, and the fur has been worn down around them; her teeth have been worn down too, though she enjoys a bone; her tail usually sports a bloodstain where she has been scratched by a thorn. She looks as if she has emerged from a fight, and so, in a way, she has.

On the sand dunes last summer she was bitten in the throat by an adder, so painfully that she howled through the night even after the vet had given her an injection. It sounded as if she were crying out, 'Oh *no*, I can't bear it.'

I did my best to hold and comfort her until dawn, when she was violently, thankfully sick. After she coughed up an awful flood of yellow, she sank down exhausted and slept. When she woke up she regained her old, slightly foolish contentment.

Recently she has been ill and I kept her in my bedroom again. Bonzo watched with a worried expression, her coat so black and eyes so bright compared to her grandmother's threadbare appearance. We took Bassey to the vet and it was obvious that she needed an operation for an infected womb. She was kept at the surgery for two days and it was doubtful whether she would return—but she did, and started hunting again.

It was too good to last and she had to go in again for an operation on another growth. When the faithful Mr Phillips brought her back, the same evening this time, she padded into the house with a glassy look of despair and headed straight for the cupboard in the corner of my bedroom, where she likes to escape.

'She's all right in herself,' said the vet reassuringly.

'There's not much of *herself* left!' I was tempted to reply. He admitted there were further growths forming inside her, but thinks she will be all right for another nine months. Her days are numbered. But she is fourteen, and age has caught up quickly. Much slower now, she is limited to short expeditions though she still responds if she scents a rabbit, and the limbs forget their stiffness. When she can manage it, she climbs clumsily into a cow's water-trough on her way back. She has always possessed a remarkable thirst; whenever I refill the bowl in my bedroom with cool fresh water, she looks up with a grateful nod before she drinks. Unlike her sister Blacky, she has been the most undemanding dog.

Though she has led a blameless life, she is entering these last days with the jauntiness of a roué. She has developed a voracious appetite as well as her habitual thirst, with a weakness for wooden spoons that have stirred cheese sauce. She found one in the kitchen as the dogs were being locked up a night or two ago, and carried it in her mouth so proudly that I felt guilty at removing it.

She is also a tea addict. In the evening, when she hears us talking around her, she thumps her tail loudly on the floor—simply pleased with life, and with the prospect of some dregs of tea.

She is given the dregs, looks up with a lop-sided grin of thanks, and licks the saucer dry.

Her tail starts thumping again, so loudly that I have to call out: 'Stop it, Bassey! Stop being so happy!'

chapter ten
A question of risk

In the anxiety to protect ourselves at any cost, even eggs have become suspect. Perhaps it is inevitable in the age of processed food, but after all these years the experts have decided that farm-yard produce is bad for us. The Royal College of Physicians—whoever they are—have issued a warning that eggs, cream and cheese are dangerous, especially egg yolks, which have 'a high cholesterol level'. Would they reduce us to scrambled *whites*? How insipid! Yet how characteristic of the blandness of today. This latest scare is particularly annoying now that our hens have started to lay, but at breakfast I shall continue to relish the golden yolks from eggs collected the night before. To hell with the experts.

I shall also resist the compulsory seat-belt in every way the law allows. Not because I hate the things, though I do. Not because I believe they are dangerous, though I have wondered about this ever since a friend skidded off a bridge and drowned, trapped inside his car.

Not even because Jimmy Savile tells me on television to belt up, though it is hard to imagine any advice less palatable.

I shall resist because this is another attempt to eliminate the risk from our lives. Restrictions are reasonable when they involve others—the breathalyser may be sordid but drunken driving is more so. A seat-belt should concern me alone.

'Wearing safety-belts is good for you,' droned the Minister for something-or-other on the television news. This has the arrogance of campaigners on pornography, who assume we do not have the wit to judge for ourselves; it is the self-righteousness of telling other people what they *ought* to do, which, I fear, is a growing English vice.

The self-appointed censors who wish to control what we read or see are as bad as the hired experts who stand up in court to declare that pornography is beautiful and positively beneficial. A curse on both their causes! I believe most pornography is stultifying, and I am sure a case can be made in favour of seat-belts— but I retain the right to be corrupted or die as I damn well please.

I enjoy a surfeit of food and drink and have no wish to be saved from myself. Warnings of coronaries try to turn me off my fresh brown eggs, but if I believed the dieticians *everything* would be bad for me. There is such hypocrisy involved. I am a non-smoker, though the government warnings tempt me to take it up; I am a drinker and realise that alcohol is just as harmful. But earnest television documentaries on the evil of cigarettes, showing old men gasping from lung cancer, are followed by commercials urging us to drink—and to drive.

'Give up smoking and it will add five years to your life,' a TV doctor assures us. What will we do with these five years—lead a compromise existence?

My mother did not smoke, yet died of cancer. My father was an addict and died, as perfectly as I could have hoped for, in a split second at home in his armchair. My mother was sitting opposite him, his dog was at his feet, his cat on his lap, and he was seventy. Doctors had advised him to stop smoking, but he was not the man to bargain for extra time without the joy of cigarettes, alcohol, or any of the risks that spelt real life to him.

'Life should not be made too sweet,' he said once. 'It can't be covered with mayonnaise.'

From my window, as the summer approaches, I can look out on two sports and hear another. The surfers are out there throughout the year, strange dark shapes in wet-suits, lying on their boards hour after hour and waiting for the right wave to bring them in. I admire, though I do not envy, their dedication in the worst of weather and the slightest of surf. From up here it seems monotonous and a bit masochistic. At least they add to the view; the sport that I *hear* contributes nothing.

Every Sunday scramblers roar up the hill beside the ravine, on their motor-bikes, churning the earth in their wake.

The third sport is wholly delightful. I can watch its participants on the top of Baggy as they prepare to take off; then the short run, and off they fly over the cliffs as free as the air that supports them. I can think of few activities such a joy to watch as hang-gliding. Undeniably, the threat of rocks below and the sea beyond add a certain zest.

I knew, the first time I saw the hang-gliders a few weeks ago, that people would try to stop them, and so they do. At first there were complaints because the gliders had accidents and died, and people cannot be allowed to go around dying as they please. Marcus Lipton MP has even recommended a ban on hang-gliding. Fortunately, the other point of view has been expressed by Chris Corston, the secretary of the British Hang-Gliding Association: 'To soar like a bird above natural and beautiful land, it's worth the risk. It's peaceful, exhilarating, wonderful. You're not closed into a hot cockpit like in a glider, you're sharing the experience of the creatures that fly.'

He continued boldly: 'We make no apologies for its being a dangerous sport. Anything that is worth doing is dangerous and hang-gliding is a risk-sport like mountain climbing or skiing.'

But the idea of living dangerously is alien to England today and objection has now been made on behalf of public safety by some district council representative, who complains that people on the ground have been kept away from a beauty spot because of the risk of accidents from pilots 'flapping overhead'. Who's flapping? From my window I can see the gliders alight on the sand as precisely as if they had stepped off a staircase.

Again the hypocrisy: why should motor-racing be tolerated and hang-gliding condemned? Could it be that speed is promoted by big business because the profits are vast?

I expect I shall still hear the din of motor-bikes on Sunday afternoons, but I wonder what the view from my window will look like in a few years' time: no dogs, because the 'scare' has succeeded and they have been banned from our beaches by Parliament; no hang-gliders; no surfers in case they should hit a swimmer—possibly no swimmers in case they drown. No canoes, for they can overturn; no rock climbers who might fall off the cliffs. At least the place will be deserted!

Absurd exaggeration—or is it? Our horror of risk could reach the point where we prefer to watch such activities on our television sets rather than in the open air 'for real'. It sounds a mean philosophy of life, but I suspect that meanness and grudging envy is part of the attitude today. This could explain the 'letters to the editor' and the criticism levelled against the horse trials at Badminton. As with foxhunting, I feel it shows less concern for the horses than resentment of the riders.

A sporting event

I had not been to Badminton before this year. HTV asked me to cover the event last year but the rain was so heavy that it was cancelled on the second day because of the damage that people and horses would inflict on the farming land. This time the weather was peerless.

I was driven from Bristol to Badminton, the home of the Duke of Beaufort, who started the trials twenty-six years ago with the aim of producing a winning team of riders for the Olympics. This has been achieved, with gold medals at Stockholm, Mexico, and Munich.

It was a modest affair to begin with, attended mostly by members of the Beaufort Hunt and a few strangers who thought they were going to watch the game of badminton (which originated there) and were startled to find themselves surrounded by horses. With the patronage of the Queen and participation by Princess Anne, the event has grown into the largest of its kind in the world. In spite of £4.50 charged for every car, 100,000 visitors can be expected for the cross-country phase on a fine Saturday. The area is large enough to contain them without any feeling of restriction; there is an atmosphere of good humour.

Several first impressions: the lines of stands that are unashamedly upper-crust. There are trade exhibits by Garrard the Crown Jewellers, offering silver salvers to celebrate Badminton's jubilee. They cost £550 'which can include up to five facsimile signatures of your choice'. I see Asprey's, with silver dogs and horses; lines of shooting sticks and rows of flat tweed caps; closed-circuit TV for your stud farm; Scottish sheepskins; dog leads and dog 'nests'; sporting tea towels, and even sticks with horse-head handles—which I thought went out of fashion with Albert. All these stands are dwarfed by the palatial line opposite of banks the height of houses, in serried splendour.

Then the dogs: more dogs than I have ever seen in a dog show, sad-eyed whippets and playful red setters, amiable labradors and ambling mastiffs, down-at-heel mongrels among the hand-made shoes, dogs resembling their owners or owners their dogs, tall dogs, small dogs, dogs of every size and shape . . . except for corgis—the most expected dog of all. Instead, the Queen clutches an affectionate long-haired dachshund called Pipkin, belonging to Princess Margaret.

This leads to the third impression—the informality of it all. The Royal Family moves freely without any noticeable posse of detectives, though I spot a burly member of the Special Branch trying to make himself invisible behind Princess Anne's Land-Rover, AMP 1. His deerstalker makes an unconvincing disguise.

Having enjoyed tea with her so often at Buckingham Palace, I am slightly disappointed when the Queen brushes past me with headscarf and stern expression, without a sign of recognition. Obviously we do not share the same dreams.

Princess Anne is a wife discussing points with her husband on horseback, before an event, with no entourage and only a courteous doffing of tweed caps. This is especially true on the day of the dressage, but the crowds are denser on Saturday and aim their cameras like a firing squad. Badminton is a unique opportunity for the photographer—the fumbling amateur and the thrusting professional. Edward Adams of *Time* magazine has flown in specially from the borders of Thailand, and appears still to be in battle-dress. Was he impressed? Not much; 'Nothing special' is his estimate, delivered with a blasé smile. 'I don't care for horses. My assignment is the Queen.'

Members of the Royal Family are easy targets for the shots of cameras or of assassins. A well-directed lob of a hand-grenade could have eliminated the Queen, the Queen Mother, Princess Margaret, Prince Philip and Prince Andrew as they sat by the water jump. Further away, completely unnoticed at another point in the course, Prince Charles circles slowly on horseback—presumably watched by invisible detectives. I wonder if he was kept apart deliberately. The sad truth is that absolute security, if there is such a thing, would be impossible at Badminton without destroying the fun.

And it is fun: a roar of good humour as Aly Pattinson is plumped smack in the lake when her horse Olivia baulks at the jump, swimming off riderless in the opposite direction before it is remounted to a sympathetic burst of applause. The inevitable eccentric, shabby-genteel in pin-stripe and a jaunty grey felt hat, which is decorated with badges and ribbons. A union jack is strapped to his umbrella and a swollen canvas bag is stuffed with sweets that he offers generously to those he talks to. A Dan Leno figure to look at, he is serious when he talks to you, relieved there have been no 'Irish outrages' to mar the event. He has wished Mark Phillips well and just had a few words with His Grace the Duke of Beaufort. Reminiscent of that other personality of music-hall, Burlington Bertie:

> I lean on some awning, while Lord Derby's yawning,
> Then he bids 'Two Thousand', and I bid 'good morning' . . .

An essential part of the canvas, he is such a fervent admirer of Badminton that he would plainly sacrifice his motley person to prevent any 'outrage', Irish or otherwise. He invites me to his home to see the replies to letters he has sent to the Royal Family and 'the late Sir Winston'. Offering me sweets, which I decline, he promises a sherry, and wanders off in search of Prince Charles to wish him well.

It is all gloriously English. The crowds stretching across the lawns in front of Badminton House, which is flying the royal standard, like a picture by Frith. The girls with Betjeman names: Jane Holderness-Roddam on Devil's Jump, Miranda Frank on Touch and Go, and Audrey Brewer on Kilkenny Brae who told me—Audrey I mean—that she had gone to a 'super' cocktail party the evening before. And of course the stunning Lucinda Prior-Palmer on Wideawake. We were lucky to find her at the stables before the dressage, dressed in a devastating rig of black boots, breeches and glistening topper. 'It helps that Mummy used to hunt and Daddy played polo, so I can use their things.' Twenty-two years old and radiant, firm-chinned with a complexion of pale honey and a hint of freckles, a head prefect in a hairnet. No wonder she is the favourite competitor, with Badminton at her feet.

On the second day, her chances suddenly improve immeasurably and we snatch a few words at the end of the cross-country. She admits breathlessly, while friends stop her with their congratulations, that she is keeping her fingers crossed for a win the next day. This would be her second Badminton win.

And she does win. Total and popular triumph as the Queen presents her with the Whitbread Trophy worth £1,000.

Then, total tragedy.

During the lap of honour, Wideawake collapses and dies instantly from a 'catastrophic haemorrhage of the brain'. Princess Anne hurries forward to comfort Lucinda, who has been thrown as the horse fell; Captain Phillips puts his arm around her. She leaves the ring, hand to her face.

Yet, in a way, this is what Badminton is all about. A question of risk again. The Duke of Beaufort has described the event as 'the greatest possible test of the strength and courage of the horse, coupled with the strength and tact of the rider'. That sums it up. Of course there was the angry protest to 'the Editor' in the *Daily Telegraph*: 'I wonder what kind of people they are who demand this limit of endurance by an animal to pander to their own vicarious triumph.' The 'kind of people' are represented by Janet Hodgson who suffered terrible injuries, and pain, at Kiev, and concussion after two falls in Germany, but was back again at Badminton on Larkspur. Thirty-three of the seventy starters failed to complete the trials, and Wideawake was not the only casualty—Harley, ridden by Sue Hatherley, had to be destroyed after damaging a tendon in the cross country.

The begrudgers raised the familiar questions: is the price for success too high? Are the fences prepared by Colonel Frank Weldon too big? Should Badminton be banned? When Lucinda Prior-Palmer recovered from her distress, she absolved Colonel Weldon immediately:

The course is designed for a brave horse. But no one who has any sympathy for or understanding of horses would ask a horse to do it unless it was in proper condition. Wideawake had jumped so brilliantly. He was ready to go again and then he died. There is just no more to say. It is one of those most unfortunate things which everyone has to bear. The fact that he died in front of thousands of people, including the Queen, has no bearing on the event. It could have happened in the stable.

Rob life of its risk, and you rob it of all adventure. Back home, she opened a bottle of champagne to toast his memory. How right! In a way it was death in the grand and gallant style—at the height of victory.

The hens . . . a last word

The month of May has seldom seemed so prolific—an epidemic of rabbits starting to decimate the vegetable garden; more wild flowers than I have ever seen here before. Drifts of blackthorn like snow as I walk up the ravine and see a hawk hovering ahead, a snake dangling from its talons like a kite on a ribbon. As always, I wish I knew more about nature.

Peter and Frances are away but an old friend has come to stay because his marriage is on the rocks again—irrevocably this time, or so it seems.

Market day in Barnstaple, Friday, which means the pubs are open all day. We lock the dogs indoors and go to take advantage of this until the day takes advantage of us. My friend says he is returning by taxi and will lock up the hens. I follow much later and the dogs seem frantic as they race outside in the dark; gradually they return and I let them stay in my room.

I wake up feeling none too jolly but prepare the mash for the hens.

A new silence as I walk up to their run: curious—their squawks can usually be heard from inside their house. Only this time they are not inside their house, and the door is still open. Their headless bodies are strewn in macabre attitudes around the run. Unnerving silence after the holocaust.

The slaughter bears all the trademarks of the fox, rather than the mink. Perhaps he has been prowling around for nights—no wonder the dogs were so desperate to be let out in pursuit.

I feel as guilty as if I had murdered the hens myself and try to off-load this onto the friend who never returned to lock them up. When I meet him later I shift my guilt so vehemently that I help to kill our friendship as well. Equally unreasonable is my change of attitude towards the fox. My earlier sympathy is over. Now that I have been victimised I regard the disdainful but adventurous animal as vermin to be hunted—a killer merely for the sake of killing. A carrier of rabies. Such is prejudice.

Fortunately, Bob Benson happens to look in that morning, helps to bury the corpses, and lifts the gloom with his usual humour.

chapter eleven

'Bit of a recluse'

I enjoy writing letters but I loathe the telephone, which starts as servant and ends as master, like the television set. Yet when I had my phone disconnected recently, I was made to feel I had committed an anti-social act.

I never liked the instrument: I resented the way it sat there in the house like an uninvited guest, always wanting something, waiting to catch me at two in the morning to plead for reassurance or mumble tearfully.

'It's urgent,' the phone would explain; urgent perhaps for 'it' but never for me. My first hint of rebellion came in the winter when a husband and wife stayed the night after dinner. Someone else's wife with someone else's husband, I should explain. No sooner in the bedroom than the woman announced she was phoning for a taxi to take her home to her own husband. It was then that her friend ripped the extension phone from the wall.

Within a few minutes they were happily in bed.

When I came down in the morning I noticed something curious—silence. Instead of the usual incessant ring, the bell was mute. I discovered I could make calls but was unable to hear the bell if anyone phoned me. It seemed the perfect arrangement. But the couple were aghast with guilt and hangover: 'I'll ring the engineers,' she said, 'and we must pay for any repairs. That's the least we can do.' I suspected she was more anxious to embarrass him than make amends to me.

'No, don't do that,' I said quickly.

'But you must have the bell repaired,' she insisted, 'so people can get in touch. We can't leave you cut off.'

'I'll see to it myself later,' I said vaguely, and made the mistake of adding: 'You see, it's so peaceful as it is.'

She tried to work this out. 'But that means you won't be able to hear us if we phone you.'

'Exactly!' I cried, before I could stop myself.

'But if you have it repaired,' she said coldly, 'you don't *have* to answer it.'

'Oh yes I do,' I assured her, 'I have no will power whatsoever.'

This is true: the sound of a phone ringing can never be ignored by me. It has always been as irresistible as the rattle of a roulette wheel, promising so much.

'Mr Fearson? Mr Daniel N. Fearson? This is TWX Chicago calling you with the sixty thousand dollar "Person-to-Person Prize" if you can name the star of——' Or Thames Television asking me to fly to Paris as one of the judges in a programme on 'The Finest Restaurants in the World' with all expenses paid and a handsome fee. Or my publisher announcing I have won an award. Even—'Come to a party, just as you are!'

It has never been like this. Instead an unfamiliar voice starts discouragingly, 'You don't know me and this is a lot to ask, but . . .' Or: 'Mr Farson? Ah, glad to find you in, this is the Westminster Bank. The Manager would like to have a word with you . . .' So the opportunity of phoning when I wanted, without being bothered in return, was ideal—except that so many people reported my phone out of order that a sleepy youth arrived one morning in a post office van.

'They say you reported your phone,' he announced glumly.

'Oh no,' I replied cheerfully, 'it's just the way I want it. Shame you had to come all this way.'

'Oughtn't you to have it fixed?' he shifted uncomfortably.

'There's no law against leaving it as it is?' I asked, for nowadays there might be. He thought hard. 'Well, there's no *law* exactly but . . .' He searched for the right words and found them surprisingly in the last line of *Hedda Gabler*, 'People don't do such things.'

The youth looked so forlorn that I relented. 'All right,' I said, 'you can fix it.' After he left, the bell rang out again instantly, as if it had been waiting.

'We've been trying to get you for *ages*,' said an accusing voice, 'but you're always out. Or you don't answer the phone. Anyhow, now we've got you, we're in your neck of the woods and thought it would be such fun if we came over tomorrow around lunchtime . . .' Who could they be?

'Of course we wouldn't have dreamt of coming without ringing you first, so I'm so glad . . .' It couldn't be Joyce Grenfell, could it? Then I remembered, the wife of a couple met once on a holiday in Crete.

'But how wonderful!' I cried, trying to sound enthusiastic.

The next day was wasted. After they had gone I thought of the calls I had missed during the taming of the bell and wondered how many would have been important to *me*. Really important, in the sense that a letter would not have arrived in time.

Apart from contact with a couple of friends, I could think of few. So when my next phone bill arrived, in three inexplicable figures, I decided to discontinue the service. 'For reasons of economy and bliss,' I explain to my friends who cannot understand it. As soon as the phone was removed, the GPO flattered me with a bombardment of leaflets. 'Not on the phone?' one of them asked incredulously. 'It's not all that expensive you know.' Since then I have been assured that 'for less than ten pence a day you can be a member of a Nationwide Club of over twelve million.'

A lavishly illustrated brochure tempts me with a choice of thirteen different instruments: 'With a telephone you can chat to friends . . . Then, of course, other people can ring you. Most of their calls will be friendly chats . . .' Ah, those friendly chats! How well I remember them, and those calls at midnight from that nice ex-actor who phoned drunkenly to talk of suicide.

I am not certain if the GPO's 'friendly chats'—like the TV trailers for forthcoming programmes—are threats or promises, but I have no doubts over my decision. The realisation that the phone is not going to interrupt me has given a new sense of peacefulness to the house. I can say truthfully that I shall forever be without one.

'Bit of a recluse, aren't you?' someone asked me in the pub the last time I was in. This is a new idea and I look it up in the dictionary at home: '(Person) given to or living in seclusion.'

Seclusion strikes me as rather a cold word; I prefer the prouder sound of solitude. But even solitude is relative and I feel ashamed of my trumpetings when I read a letter in *The Times* from Jeff and Frankie Clarkson, who have just returned to Appledore, where they live in the old Gaiety Cinema, after a five-year journey in their thirty-foot sloop. Replying to some earlier correspondence which I missed, they stress that 'the dream of so many city dwellers has no relationship to physical well-being or accident-free jobs: it is the natural longing of man for a natural environment'.

My feelings exactly, but they have put theirs to the test adventurously: 'We now know the meaning of real solitude; of dark unrelieved by sodium or any light other than natural light of moon and stars, and we know of a world which is timeless—controlled only by day and night. We have, in short, experienced the dream and know it as the meaning of the verb "to live".'

To a lesser extent I experienced the same ecstasy when I was employed as crew on a ketch that sailed for Spain from Falmouth, holding the wheel on the open deck at night-time with the stars above and the sound of the sea. I should like to add that at such a moment I understood the meaning of life, but such thoughts were distracted by the realisation that I was steering the ketch straight at a reef ahead of us, a disaster averted only by my frantic cries for help from below.

Meanwhile, I relish my own solitude, such as it is, and do not ask for whom the phone-bell tolls—for it's not for me. Now I receive a barrage of telegrams instead. A din from my dogs as the gentleman who runs the post office at Georgeham arrives in his car with his splendid Alsation looking out from the back seat, which it occupies fully. I am handed the buff envelope: 'Please call soonest urgent.' At first I used to race into the village convinced it was serious. I am learning. Like the telephone, it invariably proves more urgent for them than it does for me. I take my time now. But why do so few people write letters? These are the most welcome communication of all.

Fortunately, this is not a place where people 'drop in'. I dread the sound of a car penetrating the drive when I am at work, usually a mistaken address like those constant wrong numbers when I had the phone.

Consequently, my heart did not exactly leap with merriment when the dogs barked aggressively as a motor-bike arrived bearing a policeman in a white crash helmet that they distrusted on sight. For once I had nothing on my conscience, but I went outside warily.

It was a pleasant surprise, for this was a courtesy visit by the new police constable for Croyde and Georgeham, to introduce himself to the residents; excellent public relations and an exercise in good manners that I thought had died out years ago. His upbringing in Clovelly and his obvious regard for that way of life help to explain why he bothered. He told me what a fine place it was to grow up in, with the whole village as a playground without any danger from cars, and remembered the maroons exploding as the villagers raced down the hill to launch the lifeboat over the skids, laid like railway sleepers on the pebbles, winched via an anchor lying offshore. The first to man the boat were given a disc known as a 'dump' and received a pound for it later—'not that anyone did it for the money'.

When he was a boy the majority of the villagers had been there for generations while the new residents who had come from outside were in the minority. Now it is the other way round.

A few days after his visit I heard a car draw up, followed by strange accents and unfamiliar crimson faces as I peered round my bedroom window trying not to be seen. They saw me.

'We're after anything you might be having to sell,' announced a tall man in a vile leatherette jacket. They were modern-day tinkers, by estate car rather than horse. No clothes pegs to sell but antiques to buy. I shook my head, my hackles of suspicion rising:

what a perfect way to 'case' a lonely house and return when the owners had gone out. I stood firm at the front door, trying to make a mental note of their car number.

'Any knick-knacks,' the man continued, 'a little clock or something in the attic perhaps. Or one of those bureaux that open down. I'd give you as much as £500 for one of those—cash—if it was a good one like, cash.'

My hackles of greed overcame my suspicion. One of the 'accomplices' got out of the car and joined us. He had a real Irish face, red and tousled as if he had just woken up. Though he was younger, he appeared to be the boss.

'Whatsdat?' he pointed to the plaster cherub hanging above the door, which I had rescued from the old Metropolitan music-hall in the Edgware Road while it was being demolished around me. I took it down.

'If that had been wood, I could have given you £300—cash.'

Was he serious? This was becoming too much for me and I called to Peter and Frances for assistance; within minutes we sold a dreadful bronze doorstop of Nelson, tucked away in the garage; the china figure of a tubby sailor I had tried to sell before; and an old chair mended with fishing-line.

'How much would you offer for this?' we showed him a walnut chest-of-drawers in Peter's studio, a squat object.

'We like you to give the tax'—at least that is what it sounded like—and it went for £50. Though the tinkers were inside the house by now, I was reluctant to show them around, especially the bureau that did 'open down' in the sitting-room. Even I knew that was valuable. But they had a glimpse of the dining-room with the long oak table and wooden dresser.

'Would that be a Welsh dresser?' This was more of a statement than a question. I nodded, after all what is a dresser if not Welsh, and he offered £150. Some hurried whispers next door and the three of us agree it would be disastrous to strip the room of the very things that give it character. I was glad to lose Nelson, but these belong. The more we shook our heads the higher the offers rose, like an auction. How easy it is to bargain when you do not wish to sell.

Finally—'I tell you what, I'll give you £600 for the lot, for the table and the dresser, it's a good price.' It was, and the notes waved in front of me tempted me sorely. Then my groundless suspicion swelled again: what if the notes were forged? A final refusal—I would have surrendered to one more offer. But they were off.

Gleefully we counted the notes on the kitchen table: idiotic that a windfall or a lucky win at gambling or an unexpected sale, like this, is more satisfying than money hard-earned. Glee was followed by doubt and regret: having won such a bargain with the walnut chest, should we have sold the table and dresser as well—cash? Such is greed.

Soon I forgot about the tinkers, until this afternoon on an empty Sunday when I switched on the television and watched 'Going For a Song'. Suddenly I leaned forward: there it was—a walnut chest-of-drawers! Not mine, older and a shade more elegant, otherwise identical. Arthur Negus fussed around while I held my breath. At last he gave his expert estimate of the value—£1,200.

One thousand, two hundred pounds! Oh god! And we let ours go for fifty.

My mother and father made many homes in their lifetime: on a houseboat by the shores of a lake in British Columbia; on a boat called *The Flame*, which they sailed across Europe down the Rhine, into the Danube, and out to the Black Sea; apartments in Chicago and Berlin; and a small house in London when my father was in charge of the British bureau of the *Chicago Daily News*. When they settled in North Devon they knew it was for good.

There were no trees when they came here, only a windswept space, and their first act was to plant the pines that have grown to a handsome copse today. Then they transformed the sandy soil above the house into a garden, enclosing it with a six-foot wall. This was the first and vital windbreak against the sea gales that burn the leaves brown and bend every shrub backwards. Made by two local builders, known to my father as Jobie and Grizzleguts, it was termed a 'dry wall' though parts collapsed in the first winter rain; but they were repaired and it stands firm today.

My parents did not believe in short cuts. Arduously they double-trenched and manured the virgin earth, conscripting me

on my holidays, placing a large stone at the root of the fruit trees
that espaliered the warm west wall. It was my mother, born with
green fingers, who maintained the garden and loved it, passing
contented or at least contemplative afternoons as it grew around
her. Birches were added to the pines and birds started to make
their nests above, and once a hare in the darkness underneath.
Rows of sweetcorn reminded my father of his childhood in America, while a fruit cage that he built served as both a protection for
the currants and an aviary for the blue tits that managed to
penetrate the mesh and were caught inside.

I am no gardener—I have red fingers and no patience—but at
least I had the foresight to visit Treseders, the splendid market
garden at Truro, and order more trees and shrubs to enhance the
others. With an extravagance that for once was justified, I
planted escallonia, griselina, olearia, eucalyptus and other
shrubs whose names I have forgotten or never learnt. These have
formed a second barricade and now that the wind is deflected it is
possible to be more ambitious in such a frost-free climate with
choisya, mimosa, yucca and camellia. The fuchsia grows wild.

There is a favourite view of mine from the fields above, looking down on a solitary waving palm that seems impervious to sea-
salt, a red blaze of willow beside the stream that trickles down to
the beach, a further patch of yellow willow beside the green pines
and my *cupressus macrocarpa* that have now surpassed them,
clumps of red-hot pokers in the late spring, and the glistening
grey-slate roof of the house and the sea beyond. In the brown of
summer, from the hill above or the rowboat at sea, the many
shades of green form a small oasis.

Planting trees and seeing them grow is immensely flattering. I
am absurdly proud of one *cupressus macrocarpa* that has grown
gigantically and perfectly, as straight as a mast in defiance of the
wind. It gives me pleasure every time I pass it, but the mainten-
ance of the garden is less romantic. I tend to potter, leaving the
real work to Peter and Frances who have retrieved it from a
threatened wilderness. It has never produced so much as now.

One of the truest luxuries today is the taste of freshly picked
vegetables—even peas seem old and battered by the time they
reach the shops—not so much the brief reign of asparagus as the
simplest spring greens, which are incomparable when you can

pick them as you choose; beans and marrows while they are young and firm, and not yet swollen into the competitive giants beloved by British flower shows.

As with life, the greater the participation the stronger the flavour; this may not be logical but the feeling of achievement makes it so, with new potatoes that have to be dug, peas podded, fruit picked and peeled, currants topped and tailed, or an onion grown miraculously from seed. These are a whole experience away from the fake and artificial flavourings (not flavours) of today, epitomised by monosodium glutamate, a suitably unlovely name for such a deceiving ingredient.

At this moment of the year, however, there is a lull. Everything is in abeyance though the buds are bursting on the fruit trees. Potatoes and onions have been planted but do not show; the invasion of rabbits has eluded the snares and eaten the young lettuce and cabbage; and though the broad beans are rising tall, the only vegetables to pick are the ever faithful spinach and the curly greens that nobody seems to like, not even the devastating pigeon.

This tempts me to experiment. I have heard so much about the delicacy of young nettle-tops that I collect a bagful from the copse where they grow profusely among the goosegrass, and make nettle soup. I prepare and blend it as for spinach, and take a suspicious sip. Interesting! Adding a few drops of lemon juice to lighten a slight mustiness, I decide it is excellent. Later I realise it is perfectly adequate but not sufficiently exciting to try again.

Sorrel is another matter, so plentiful that I have taken it for granted as a weed until last year when I discovered its value. The taste is similar to spinach, but has an extra sharpness—a hint of lemon—and the leaves melt so easily that it makes a perfect sauce to go with fish; or a purée; or, best of all, a cheese-and-sorrel soufflé. Just as certain herbs enhance a meat or vegetable—tarragon with chicken; basil with tomato—sorrel is the perfect complement to cheese.

Obviously, this is another reward of living here—the satisfaction of growing my own food or collecting it for free. Mussels and cockles from the estuary now; wild mushrooms and blackberries in September. Sometimes the dogs contribute a rabbit, snatched away before they tear it to pieces among themselves. I have no compunction in letting them hunt, for rabbits are hardly an endangered species around here: they have recovered from that vile man-made myxomatosis. For one rabbit caught, ten thousand get away.

Soon comes the summer day when I look out from my window, see an agitation of seagulls above a rippling patch of sea, and know the mackerel are in. This can be tantalising when the surf is too high to launch the rowboat, but there will be days when it is possible to race down to the beach, drag the boat across the sand and row out frantically to the spot—only to find the shoal has moved on. Then I row wildly in pursuit, sight them again and row right through them, but the fish are too close to the surface for spinners, or they are not biting, or they are not mackerel at all but grey mullet. These are infuriating, surrounding the boat, their fins breaking the surface so it is almost possible to scoop them out by hand, but they refuse to bite. On sultry evenings they move close to the shore like yellow-brown slicks. Last year, when they hovered opposite Vention Cottage, Jack Boucher was delighted when a sanitary inspector arrived to take a sample of the water, convinced that it was an outlet for sewage. Refusing to believe Jack's explanation, he was mystified when his test revealed nothing. The best, probably the only way to catch these mullet is to wade out with a seine net and haul them in with the help of several companions. Jack remembers catching 150 lb. in a single netting, while a record catch in Croyde Bay reached seven cwt. Vention corner is also noted for salmon peel and bass, pronounced 'barss' round here. At the close of one unsuccessful night, Jack and his friends suddenly netted a complete sackful of 'barss', about thirty of them.

Not having a net, I am content with the rowboat. More than content. There was an epic occasion a few years back when we caught more than 150 mackerel in an afternoon, though the triumph was marred by an inability to dispose of them fast enough. Now that we have a deep-freeze waiting for such a glut, the mackerel have become scarcer. Perhaps the accusations of over-fishing by trawlers are correct. Now it is more the luck of catching solitary mackerel rather than landing a shoal, but the satisfaction is infinite. It is a happy exhaustion rowing back in the evening, watching the lines of surf anxiously as they build up on the shore. It is necessary to row in backwards for the last fifty yards or so to avoid capsizing, which would mean the loss of the silver shapes turning green and mauve at the bottom of the boat. I find few fish so delicious as mackerel. Grilled with butter and Dijon mustard, or smoked over oak dust in a biscuit tin and then grilled lightly before serving, or made into fishcakes with grated onion, mashed potato and herbs from the garden, the versatility of the fish is extraordinary and the British even more so for despising them.

Not that the reward of food is needed for the relaxation of rowing alongside Baggy Point. There is a perfect peace so close to the water with no distraction of engines, just the hush as cormorants cross above or the useless indignation from gulls scattered about the rocks.

The rowboat has given me as much fun as the turbo-jet speedboat I used to own, but that was a different kind of fun, with the thrill of racing over Bideford Bar to Appledore, or crossing to Clovelly and tying up at the quay for a drink at the Red Lion. With no propellers it was possible to navigate the most unlikely stretches but as it weighed a ton, literally, such journeys were fraught; especially when I thought it odd to see gulls walking Christ-like on the water and a moment later struck an invisible sandbank. Then the glow, inside and out, after wading ashore, with the long walk beside the Pill and the prospect of a drink at The Mariners, the first pub in Braunton. And all the way back again when the tide turned, to float it off. Of course that is the joy of boats, the unexpected mishap as much as the smooth journey: the narrow escape at the Bar when the engine failed; the humiliation of being rescued by lifeboat, faces burnt from the reflected sun and hair stiff with salt. When the sun shone, the engine worked and the tides were right, the speedboat was a beauty skimming over the corrugated surface of the estuary, but this coincidence was rare. The boat was intended for freshwater lakes or broad rivers, not the corroding ocean. With no slipway or mooring nearer than Braunton Pill, the difficulty of pushing a trailer weighing a ton through the soft sand and the impossibility of launching it when the surf was high, the boat was sadly impractical. As for the chance of steering it into the bay and beaching it below the house on an ebbing tide when the sea was as flat as glass, I had to accept that such days happened once or twice a year—apart from the incredible summer of '76. On a magical evening when the sea merged into the skyline, I learnt that the stillness was usually the false calm before the storm and the weather would change completely the next day. The good spell would be over and the boat at the mercy of a violent sea if it had been left below. But on the one occasion when a storm broke unexpectedly, when I was returning from Lynton, the boat saved my life. The water fell on me with such force that I could hardly see, but the engine never faltered and we reached the safety of Ilfracombe Harbour before it sank.

Finally, I sold it. And see it now occasionally, with much nostalgia, at Ilfracombe. I have only the rowboat now. At least the slower, feebler engine—myself—is more reliable, and better too for fishing.

I expect my father would have despised the speedboat, but I regret he never knew the satisfaction of the rowboat. For he was a king of fishermen: this is why he bought the Grey House. In my foreword to a recent reprint of his classic *Going Fishing*, I wrote:

> Whenever his life was falling apart, and that was surprisingly often, my father packed his trout rods and escaped. When I was eight years old he resigned from his job with the *Chicago Daily News* and we set out across Europe in our battered Ford. It was a terrible journey. But the moment we reached the lake in the far north of Yugoslavia, everything was different. We unpacked all our trunks, not just for the single night, and the rods were put together.
>
> My father found himself again: 'Fishing those streams was my Nirvana,' he wrote years later. 'A short time after I was in the stream my mind was miles away from it, in another world. In this mood, letting my mind wander freely, I had moments when I was as close to some of the intuitive truths as any Hindu practising Yoga. There was the water, pure as the snows from which it came; the beech and alder in spring bud as the world began to renew itself; the steady rocks ripping the flow into a dancing white rapid; and up above, where the dark pines stood over a deep pool, a bend around which lay another lovely prospect. Here was the grace of life.'

The royalties from *Going Fishing* paid for this house, and it is easy to imagine how his hopes soared when he settled here—all this water!

> I bought it, [he wrote] because of the fishing. For if ever I saw a stretch of sand and sea that is a surf-caster's dream, we have it. Hardy's made me a beautiful greenheart rod, American pattern; a friend in the Embassy got me over a superb Van Hofe reel. My publishers, who were used to putting their authors into hospitals or asylums, sent me over the full list of what I had asked them to buy from Abercrombie & Fitch—cuttyhunk line, bloc-tin squids, three-way swivels, 4-oz pyramidal sinkers, three-ply casts [I am using the American nomenclature] etc., etc.; the same line of tackle that I had used when I was twelve years old, and bought from the same company. I could almost retire on the money I have spent during a lifetime at Abercrombie & Fitch: to walk through that store is an emotional debauch.'

And all for nothing as far as North Devon was concerned; far from cuttyhunk line or pyramidal sinkers, he would have done better with a bamboo cane and a bent pin. The fiasco gradually became apparent:

> The British fish were too conservative; they had never heard of these American gadgets. For two desperate years, night and day, I fished the sea right in front of our house. No fish. A few spotted sand-sharks gave themselves up, the type they call 'nurse'; fine for the cats, but my wife, who does not like their sweet taste, declared that one of them turned in the frying pan and stared at her . . .
>
> I can't describe my dismay. And I am absolutely certain that if I had been able to do my bit of surf-casting every day, wading out into the sea to plunk a 4-oz sinker beyond the waves; or better still, if I could have worked a squid through the sea the way I used to do for bluefish—and I love doing that every bit as much as fly-casting—I should never have begun to wade in those oceans of alcohol that I then began to take aboard. To stick it out, and not just pull up anchor and try to live somewhere else, was one of the hardest bits of moral discipline I have made myself face.

What went wrong? It is poignant and baffling to read these words, for the fish were there. Not only the mackerel beyond, but splendid sea-bass in the surf. With his skill, my father could have cast a few yards from our steps when the tide was high—it would have been that easy. If he had known this, his heart would have leapt as wildly as the fish.

The explanation is painfully simple: he used the wrong bait. Usually the least gadgety of men, he overrated the simple tastes of the local fish and for all his experience he failed to realise that the favourite lure of the sea-bass is ordinary lugworm dug from the Taw and Torridge Estuary near the White House.

Local people remember seeing my father on the beach, sitting on an up-turned box with the glow of his constant cigarette marking him as darkness fell, until he gave up and climbed the steps back to the house, disillusioned. It seems so strange that none of them mentioned the bass or brought lugworm for him, but surf-casting was not their style of fishing.

Some years after my father's death, Anthony Pearson came to stay here. He arrived with a copy of his book *Successful Shore Fishing*, inscribed 'Negley was an inspiration. His book is still the finest', and at dusk he clambered down the steps with Peter to take advantage of a high September tide. Within an hour they returned excitedly with five glistening silver bass, as beautiful as any salmon. Delighted for us, I felt a twinge of regret for my father. The fish had been there all the time.

chapter twelve

The dreaded saturation point

The invasion started imperceptibly; suddenly it is overwhelming. Lulled by winter into a false sense of solitude, I am taken by surprise as the hordes descend on the sands below. To resent such people on holiday would be mean and self-defeating: tourism is something I have to accept.

The worst problems from now on are the lanes that will become choked with cars, many of whose drivers seem unable to reverse. Yet if the lanes were widened it would be worse, opening the way for coaches and charabancs. Choked or not, the winding lanes are part of the character of the place.

At least one of us is delighted to see the cars pouring down the hill to the car park at the end of the Bay. This is Pencil, who welcomes the cars, literally.

Can dogs go pleasantly mad? There are times when I wonder about her.

Pencil has always been a loner, setting out on her own to be greeted ecstatically by the other dogs when she returns. While they clutch her long grey muzzle with their teeth she stands still, resigned to the penalty for being royal.

When she was younger she attached herself to a family on the sands with such an air of grief that they assumed she was lost, especially when she jumped into their car. Fortunately, a disc round her slender neck and a few enquiries revealed otherwise, but I found it slightly embarrassing when she was brought back and stared at me as if she had never set those tragic eyes on me before. Holding her in my arms I waved a paw fatuously as her friends departed reluctantly and she looked after them pleadingly, as if she had been consigned to dogs' Dachau.

As soon as their car disappeared and I put her down, she wriggled on her back delightedly and jumped up to kiss me frantically. A fine actress.

Looking down from my window in the summer, I watch her progress across the beach as she picks a group to sit by. Occasionally I see them shoo her away unpleasantly and she wanders off, tail down dejectedly, but not for long. Most people are touchingly pleased by her adoption of them, even sending her cards at Christmas with colour 'snaps'. Perhaps it is a memory of this that makes her act so strangely now. She slept all winter as if every day was a final effort, but I realise that she was hibernating. Now, as if reporting for work, she trots off to the car park where she sits all day, occupying the solitary chair in the kiosk where the attendant hands out the tickets and collects the money. Luckily he has taken to her, though she stops him sitting down, and he buys her a bar of chocolate at eleven. Perhaps, like the families on the beach, he is gently flattered. So she sits there, gradually becoming covered with dust from the passing cars, though at least she does not hear the din. Until I told him, the attendant had not realised she is totally deaf.

'Ah,' he said, 'that explains why she never notices when people call out "Pencil" as they go by. Everyone seems to know her.'

Soon after four in the afternoon she returns to the house in a state of dusty delirium, accepts her usual ovation from the others, drinks immensely, and passes out on her blanket. If we are out walking, she scents our track, nose to the ground like a hoover and follows in pursuit. I have watched her doing this from only a few yards away, behind a hedge, but she did not hear me and was too intent on her particular trace. What a curious fantasy world she lives in.

Though it is a second home to her, the car park is an eyesore in the summer. But natural resentment is tinged with financial envy. Most of the land around here belonged to Pickwell Manor, including the end field and my own house, which was built in 1933 or thereabouts by Pickwell's owner, Major Styles, for his brother-in-law who acted as agent. When the land was sold, Pickwell Manor became a hotel and the corner field was bought by Lady Robertson, of Putsborough Manor, who used it as a private bathing beach. When she left, she offered the field to the few residents along the lane in order to keep it undeveloped; the sum she was asking was reputedly £1,000. Incredibly, the residents, including my father and mother, turned it down. Stanley Tucker of Putsborough Farm had the common-sense to buy it instead. Now it must take almost that amount from the cars alone on an August Bank Holiday.

To put the record straight, providing a car park was never Mr Tucker's objective: the police asked if he would make the field available when people started to park in the lanes and block them. In fact it is extremely fortunate that it belongs to a farmer who lives for the land as well as from it. While another purchaser might have developed, he maintains. The last time we met he was going to considerable trouble to find a traditional thatcher with the right machinery to restore the roof of his splendid old farmhouse next to Putsborough Manor. His son Steven works the land with him, and Jeanne his daughter rides her horse in winter and looks after the beach shop below the car park in summer. After her marriage it will be run by Steven's wife, Stephanie.

They may be the new rich—farmers in possession of land that has become hugely valuable—but their love of the land is inherited too and I would rather have them than anyone else. My only regret is that no one thought of the field behind the skyline for the car park. Admittedly people would have to walk a couple of hundred yards down to the sea, but the view would have been enhanced at the end of it. And if they preferred to sit in their car with the window up and the radio on it would be nobody's loss. We are making everything too easy.

A report by the Dartmoor National Park in 1976 stated that 70 per cent of people who stop their cars walk less than a mile, and that 40 per cent did not venture further than a hundred yards. The National Park Committee complains that 'visitor pressure [has] an impact on soil and vegetation which in extreme cases leads to erosion and the consequent unsightly appearance on the scene which was the original attraction'. In other words, the mess of toilets and caffs and plastic cups. One solution is not to encourage this by laying everything on, except for people who are disabled. Do not provide transport for every yard, or concrete shelters on the moors in case of rain. There is the frightful prospect of 'listening-posts' dotted across the West Country, for visitors to plug themselves in to hear commentaries on local beauty spots. The Countryside Commission (of all bodies) proposes that 'once the listening-posts go into general use in England and Wales people will be able to buy their own stethoscopes . . . to carry with them in their cars and plug in anywhere in the countryside'. This was reported by Peter Simple in the *Daily Telegraph* on 17 June 1976 and he went on to comment: 'I am assuming (and it is surely not too much to assume) that the use of these posts, at first voluntary, will eventually be made compulsory by law with a corps of listening-post wardens to ensure that nobody threatens environmental conformity and public order by neglecting to use them.' The reality is bad enough. Like Americans in their drive-in cinema, the visitor need never leave his car provided it contains a portable toilet too. He can be told where to go and what to see and how to appreciate it. Far from being seen by the beholder, beauty will be translated on tape. Can our vicariousness go further? Even 'home-movies' are filmed on the family's initiative, and not supplied.

Let them get out and walk, and see for themselves—and get soaked to the skin if it is raining.

At least the Tuckers have refused to allow kiosks and ice-cream vans; their beach shop is a well-run family business; and the corner of Vention remains unspoilt when the visitors leave.

I cannot even resent Putsborough Sands Hotel on top of the hill. Though the new extensions stand squatly against the skyline, old photographs prove it was never a lovely building. Inside it has been transformed, largely because it too is a family business. Mr and Mrs Drayton and their sons are able to give the personal enthusiasm it needs. In today's perverse society, hard-earned profit is a rarity, but it makes all the difference to the customer when the people who look after you know it is to their advantage too. The bar commands one the most dramatic panoramas in Britain; the food is excellent, according to people who have stayed there—mainly young couples with children.

So what am I complaining about? Not much. It annoys me a little that summer visitors, who used to arrive on the beach after ten and leave before six, are already setting up their wind-breaks if I go for a solitary swim at eight in the morning, and linger in the evening until dusk.

But this is selfishness. My one concern is the danger of reaching a saturation point after which everything will be destroyed for everyone, especially the tourists who come here for the peace and beauty of the place. Pass this saturation point and the tourist industry will be committing suicide.

I am not protesting that the coastline *has* been saturated, I am anxious that we should keep it as unspoilt as it is today. For this is still the staggering truth of the West Country: small parts may be choked with cars or stained by caravans, but vast areas remain natural.

You realise this on a train journey from Barnstaple to Exeter. The seats are hard and the heat turned on full, regardless of the temperature outside, but I should miss it if they discontinue the line as they threaten to do and have done already between Barnstaple and Taunton. Apart from the inconvenience, I should miss the pre-war flavour of the train drawing to a halt at night in the middle of nowhere to allow a lady to alight and disappear into the undergrowth.

The track runs beside the River Taw, with pine forests reminiscent of those of the Alps. In the early morning you can see the wildlife as the mist rises, heavy herons lifting off wearily from the river bank. In the late spring the wild flowers are complemented by the cared-for gardens of the small railway halts—they can hardly be described as stations—festooned with wistaria and roses.

Or that exciting curve round the sea after Exeter, on the way to Plymouth. If you have travelled from the north it is a dreary business until Exeter, when it becomes one of the most exhilarating train journeys in Europe, especially if you are in the restaurant car next to the window with the passing glow of the early evening outside. After a few minutes the sea races into view: people bathing, children waving, a dog cavorting unrestrainedly; fleets of small boats as the train rattles through Teignmouth, three boys fishing, a flight of birds skimming the calm water.

'Kids from the Midlands must go mad when they see this!' I exclaimed to the buffet-car attendant one evening.

'If they see someone drowning, sir,' came the dampening reply. But for me, at least, this journey is spectacular.

Or take the back road, which is always the most rewarding way to travel, from here to Taunton over Exmoor and the country of Lorna Doone through Simonsbath and Exford, where brown trout quiver in the stream that runs through the village. Beyond the Brendon Hills to Bridgwater, where a motorway madness brings everything to a squealing halt, but until then there has been a constant contrast of crouching trees on windswept moors with the sudden tundra descent into wooded valleys such as Lynmouth.

Or, best of all, take a bicycle down forgotten tracks or strike out on foot and cross the country at random as people used to do. Then you will glimpse the West Country as it must have been when cars were rare and driving an adventure. Even a hint of those untarnished days when there were no cars at all, but a train to bring the visitor near his destination, with a horse to take him from there.

Today 77 per cent of holiday visitors arrive in the West Country by car and it is prophesied that the M5 motorway will be able to bring more than ten million people from the Midlands in three hours. A Birmingham businessman could race down to Devon for an afternoon's golf.

No harm in that, except that by making it too easy in the first place we shall make it impossible in the end. Inevitable bottlenecks will lead to more open spaces stolen for caravan sites and wider roads. Like the surgeon's knife, once they start cutting they seldom stop.

Better to prevent the disease in the first place, or concentrate it in certain areas, but we are making the mistake of dispersing it, which means the countryside will be tamed all over. The coastline should be sacred, but already there is a frightening indication of what may happen to the Marine Drive above the bay. Following a recommendation by the Devon County Council to extend the road to take more cars, the *North Devon Journal* of 7 October 1976 quotes a protest from the Georgeham Parish Council which implies, alarmingly, that it is not an extension at all but a through road:

> to link with Vention [which] might bring some measure of relief to the road through Georgeham, but the prospect of Woolacombe and Croyde joined by a length of parked cars was 'dire' indeed. Add to that the inevitable 'improvement' in the form of road surfacing, lighting, toilets, and refreshment kiosks and it will become a violation of a magnificent stretch of land and the widespread wish to keep it so.

Ever the optimist, I suspect that someone has made a mistake somewhere, for a through road would lead to the very congestion they seek to prevent and which does *not* exist along the Marine Drive now. It stretches for several miles from Woolacombe above the bay, coming to a stop a few fields away, and I have yet to see cars parked solidly along it even on an August Bank Holiday. Perhaps some planner dreamt this up on paper, like the modern architect who fails to visit the site of his design. I do not need to live here to recognise that such a through road would produce an explosion of cars and then coaches so they would *have* to widen the road, which will then stay wider forever.

In fact, the proposal to connect the Marine Drive 'with the National Trust lands at Vention Cottages, and open up the area for temporary parking' was made in the North Devon Coast Study published in July 1976 as an 'examination of recreation and tourism in Woolacombe, Croyde and Saunton'. It caused such anxiety that a meeting was arranged early in 1977 by the Croyde Area Residents' Association to meet members of the Devon County Planning Department at the Croyde Village Hall. Largely due to the frankness of Peter Hunt, the Assistant County Planning Officer, and the tactful chairmanship of Jeremy Thorpe, the meeting was surprisingly constructive. Peter Hunt gave a promise that in view of the opposition locally the Marine Drive would not be extended. When I asked about a proposed picnic area on the site of the burnt out Heathercombe Hotel on the hill above me, I was told that this was nullified without the extension of the Drive. Several strong opinions were aired: one resident complained that Croyde had been declared an area of natural beauty, yet, in sixteen years, had become one of 'unnatural ugliness' in summer, but most people left the meeting feeling that the planners were more sympathetic and reasonable than expected. So did I, yet a further look at the Study suggests a determination to plan for planning's sake—a fatal dispersion instead of a concentration on places already developed. Only a month or two after the meeting, a work force has started to clear gorse above the Marine Drive with the obvious intention of making paths and possibly a picnic area. Yet this whole bay is a picnic area! There is no need for benches or clearings.

I had the luck to meet Peter Hunt socially before the meeting, though I was unaware of his official position then. Discussing the subject generally, and a proposal to have an extended car park in the middle of the Marine Drive to allow people to go down to the middle of the sands more easily, I stressed my own resistance to just such a policy. At the height of summer, most people are content to cluster together at opposite ends of the beach as if an invisible line had cordoned them off. The majority prefer this. A few want a greater degree of solitude and are prepared to make the extra effort of walking a mile or two further on. This seems a perfect balance to me. By making such a car park, or drive-down, by clearing picnic areas and installing benches, 'beach accesses and toilet facilities, suitably boarded', the planners will persuade holidaymakers to descend everywhere, taming the whole of the coastline. Ultimately this will benefit no one, but by then it will be too late to reverse the trend. As 120,000 day trippers flooded this area in a single week in August 1974, it needs little imagination to see how easily this could happen.

I raised this vital 'saturation point' with John Fowler, the head of the North Devon Tourist Association, on a television programme a few years ago. He replied that he thought it would be 'all right in our lifetime' which enabled me to strike a self-righteous attitude, saying that future generations will curse us if we throw this chance away of protecting *their* heritage.

Pompous stuff but I believe it is true, that we should think in terms of fifty or a hundred years from now. If not, your grand-children will appreciate the charm of North Devon through faded photographs and the memories of old people.

The North Devon Tourist Association was started by John Fowler himself. You or I could have done so if we had had the in-itiative, and Mr Fowler would be less than human if he was not encouraged by the John Fowler Holiday Villages which he runs successfully at Ilfracombe and Westward Ho! He makes the reasonable point that Ilfracombe suffers from exceptionally high unemployment and depends on tourism for survival. At first this seems unanswerable. Obviously hotels, boarding-houses, gift shops and the like depend on it absolutely, but I wonder if the general gain is as great as people think. Nowadays, people coming to caravans or self-service flats bring most of their food with them from their own shops back home, rather than buy pro-visions here. Conversely, where the potential profit is good enough the supermarkets move in and the small shop benefits even less.

There is the disadvantage also that the summer invasion cor-rodes the community life of the town making Ilfracombe re-semble a ghost town in winter. To some degree this is inevitable with a seaside resort—not that I am against resorts for a moment. On the contrary! They are the vital shock-absorbers for tourism and should be encouraged to the hilt. I only wish that Ilfracombe was better at it. People talk disdainfully of the risk of another 'Blackpool', but Blackpool is splendidly robust in its own right. The trouble is that Ilfracombe has lost its identity. It is a town in abeyance, uncertain what it wants to be. A breath-taking opportunity is there, if only someone has the imagination to see it and the will to seize it.

chapter thirteen

The seaside resort

Oh, I love to sit a-gyzing on the boundless blue horizin,
When the scorching sun is blyzing down on sands, and ships, and
  sea!
And to watch the busy figgers of the happy little diggers
Or to listen to the niggers, when they choose to come to me!

F. Anstey

The resort was a glorious and essentially a British invention.
The prospect of 'a day by the seaside' still conjures up the childhood excitement of a treat—a spree—an outing. The resort was
an eccentric combination of innocence and elegance, with
Punch and Judy on the sands and the Nigger Minstrels celebrated in the verse above, which would doubtless be banned by

the Race Relations Board if distributed today. These were flanked by a grand array of hotels like palaces, arcades and aquariums.

People talk of Dr Brighton, but the resort was created at Scarborough even though it started as a spa. In 1626 a 'gentlewoman' tasted the spring water and found it so filthy she assumed it must be medicinal. As 'The Queen of English Watering Places' prospered, our finest architects contributed to the lustre of the town: Thomas Verity with the Spa Buildings, Henry Wyatt with a Gothic Saloon, Paxton with a concert hall. The spa turned into a resort and when the railway came in 1846 it brought thousands of northern workers who were able to escape from 'the smell of oil and the clank of the steam hammer'. If it rained, they could run indoors and enjoy themselves in a People's Palace which offered grottoes, models of Niagara and New York, an oriental theatre, an Arcadian Fun Palace, or a Floral Hall. The resorts aimed high from the outset.

Ilfracombe was one of the earliest. At first this seems astonishing: 203 miles from London and 263 from Manchester, Ilfracombe could hardly have been less accessible before the late arrival of the railway in 1874. Yet in 1851 Ilfracombe had been listed officially as one of eleven resorts, with Brighton, Ramsgate, Margate, Worthing, Weymouth, Scarborough, Ryde, Cowes, Dover and Torquay.

The first train had reached Torquay three years earlier, welcomed by the inhabitants with three cheers and a public holiday. By 1859, as many as 73,000 passengers took the train from London to Brighton in a single week. As Chesterton put it, the seaside resort had become 'the great gusto of the age'. By 1871, forty-eight resorts were listed and the number grew rapidly.

Ilfracombe's early popularity is easily explained: with one of the finest natural harbours in Europe, the visitors were brought by steamship across the Bristol Channel—from Bristol, Cardiff, Swansea and other towns on the South Wales coast.

Ilfracombe was originally a small fishing village with a single street, yet it was able to send six ships to help Edward III's expedition against France in 1346, when Liverpool could only muster one. There was a famous occasion that allegedly took place in 1797, when four French ships anchored offshore, preparing to

invade, and a farmworker called Betsy Gammon marshalled all
the women to line the cliffs in their red petticoats. Mistaking
them for a force of soldiers, the French sailed off again. The museum in Wilder Street, delightfully cluttered with every sort of
object, has fascinating pictures which show the gradual changes,
but the old prints and photographs do not reveal the atmosphere
of a foreign port and there is precious little evidence today. The
most vivid description comes in a charming, guileless booklet
called *Ilfracombe's Yesterdays* by Lilian Wilson, who is in her
eighties now and recalls, in her turn, the memories of an old lady
who was ninety-four in 1932 and told her about the Irish ships
that brought cattle for sale and the women who pitched their
tents on the Strand, cooking their meals in iron crocks over open
fires. Local men helped unload the cattle, which were hoisted up
with sacking and thrown overboard to swim ashore:

> People living near would put up their shutters and bolt their
> doors as many of the animals were wild and savage, bulls
> sometimes causing injury and damage. At times the town
> would be full of foreigners, Frenchmen, Turks, Indians and
> Africans and other races, when big ships carrying loads of
> nuts and bound for Bristol would put into the harbour be-
> cause of stormy weather. Later, perhaps because of lack of
> wind, they might be in the harbour for days. Often their be-
> haviour caused fights and much trouble.

Mrs Wilson herself remembers as many as six paddle-steamers
tied up to the pier, belonging to the Red and White Funnel Companies which were in fierce competition:

> Once my father was driving my pony Fairy in a trap along the
> Pier Road just as some day trippers were coming off the White
> Funnel steamer. As usual they were all full of high spirits and
> many had been drinking on board. They would climb the pier
> gates and refuse to pay the toll which was only a penny. One
> of the men trippers hit Fairy, which was a silly and dangerous
> thing to do as there were no railings along the road edge.
> Though Father told the man to stop, he did not, so Father
> jumped out and threw him in the harbour. *That* stopped him
> and the others that were shouting and frightening the pony.
> Some jumped in themselves to save the man but as none of

them could swim the sailors had to fish them all out—I believe a good time was had by all the onlookers. In the meantime, Father had taken the pony and trap back to the stables.

I remember the sergeant of police coming up and asking if Father was at home. Mother said 'No', so he said, 'Tell Bill to keep out of my sight until tomorrow.' When he told her why, naturally she was worried but he said, 'Don't worry, they are leaving on the late night boat. I shall report that I cannot find him.' Of course, I thought my Dad a hero and that it served the man right.

Ilfracombe became fashionable. An elegant arcade was lined with high-class shops. People took a pride in the place and built arches of ferns and flowers when there was something to celebrate, such as a royal event.

As early as 1836, tunnels were built to the sea to compensate for Ilfracombe's one drawback—a lack of sand. When John Fowler started his recent competition to name the coastline, the most popular entry was 'Coast of Sands' until people realised that Ilfracombe has no sands, so they called it 'The Golden Coast' instead. But in those early days two tunnels reached special bathing pools built into the sea, one for gentlemen, the other 'a retired cave to the right, which is set apart for the especial accommodation of ladies. Here, as the tide retires, it leaves a large basin of sea water, called the Ladies Bathing Pool, where the most timid may enjoy themselves at all seasons.' (*Health Resorts* by Spencer Thomson, 1860)

'Donkeys pulled their bathing huts to the water's edge, to spare the ladies immodesty and to deprive the gentlemen of a moment's titillation.' So much so that a bugler used to sit on a rock dividing the two pools and would blow a blast if he saw a man creeping round. Mrs Wilson says the bathing boxes were like small rooms on iron wheels, with portable steps leading up to the door:

> No lady would think of walking down the beach to the water. In fact I do not think she would have been allowed to do it! All you saw of the bathers was when they were in the water. Just before the First World War you still wore your bathing dress to your neck and to below your knee. You did sit on the rocks around the pool in between a swim but you did *not* sit on the

beach or walk around in a bathing dress as they do now.

The pools were eaten away by storms and mixed bathing briefly shocked the town, but at least the Bath House entrance remains and the tunnels are managed by a private company.

The early elegance was enhanced by the Victorian Pavilion, built of glass on iron frames with money raised from public funds. A photograph taken at the turn of the century shows what an attractive place it must have been for sitting in, shaded by creepers, lined with hundreds of plants in pots, with palm trees growing down the centre. There was an aquarium and a concert stage where companies charged for the seats in front while a collection was taken from the people standing behind; it was somewhere to listen to music in winter and to seek refuge from a glaring sun or sudden shower in summer.

Then the council thought it would be more profitable to cut it in two, and rebuilt the façade in 1924. This set the pattern for the future of Ilfracombe.

Today Ilfracombe may seem in need of one really luxurious hotel, like the Imperial in Torquay or the wedding-cake Carlton in Bournemouth. It had one: the Ilfracombe Hotel opened in 1861 with 250 bedrooms at four guineas a week, and the reputation that guests needed a title to stay there. Rather grandiloquently it was described as 'the gathering place for Royalty in the Victorian era', which may have been a reference to Prince Wilhelm who spent a holiday at the hotel with his tutor. One morning a boy called Alfred Price was helping his father to move some bathing machines when he spotted the Prince throwing stones at them, whereupon Alf rushed over, punched him in the nose and knocked him down before the tutor could intervene. Perhaps the future Kaiser was involved in several fights, for another version mentions a young fisherman called Barbeary. The name is still pre-eminent today: the White Hart on the quay is run by Tom Barbeary, and 'Barbeary's' is the first-rate fishmonger behind the harbour which gets supplies from its own trawler.

Most resorts sprang to life because of the railway, like Newquay which suddenly became a nine-hour journey from London. Railways were the rage and the gentry stayed in the

Great Western Hotel near Newquay station while their servants rented houses nearby.

It shows how solidly Ilfracombe was established that the town did not have to wait for the railway before building its grand hotel. But when the first trains did arrive in 1874 the town lost the chance of becoming as grand a resort as Torquay. Mrs Wilson records that:

> The Great Western Railway wanted to buy [the recently constructed pier] but the Council stopped the deal, which was a very foolish thing to do. If the railway had bought it they intended running their own line from Minehead to Ilfracombe and to sail passenger and goods boats to Wales and Bristol etc. in connection with the railway. Instead, the G.W.R. had to share the existing line at the top of Station Hill with the London South Western. To have two railways in competition with each other would have been very good for the town; it has always been said it was the railways that made Torquay. I am afraid my father had not much faith in council ways.

Even so, the railways brought the day-tripper from inland, to complement the steamers, and Ilfracombe's exclusiveness was lost. This was inevitable, but Mrs Wilson noted that 'The growth of the day-tripping and holiday industry quite changed the town's character. It drove away the good class families that provided the better shops with a living. Now it is very much a working-class town. The houses where the rich lived have been turned into hotels, boarding houses and bed-and-breakfast places.'

Astonishing how the circle turns: writers were already lamenting the decline of Ilfracombe in the last century. One acknowledged the improvements—£30,000 spent on drains, £50,000 on bringing water from Challacombe—prophesying, 'Ilfracombe will become more popular, more cosmopolitan, more gay; its resemblance to London will be more marked and its jollity downright continental.' This was not intended as a compliment, for he continued: 'To old-fashioned people this mania for commercial progress, this pandemonium of extravagant revelry is anathema.'

I have found an old guide-book published in 1895 which

deplored the 'inevitable cocknefying which everywhere, nowadays, overtakes the fashionable watering place. Alas! and alas!'
Even then they were starting to lament. The author, John Lloyd
Warden Page, complained of the penny tolls that had to be paid
to the private owners if you wished to walk along the Torrs above
the town, but he had it both ways when he added, 'They serve to
keep out the commonest of the common trippers, so let us pay our
oboli and be thankful.' I can only hope that my own comments
will not seem so snobbish in a hundred years' time. Neither did
Mr Page approve of the attractions waiting when you reached
the top: 'a large glass refreshment house surrounded by a brist-
ling array of automatic machines—vulgo, "penny in the slots".'
Already, he was thinking wistfully of the good old days

> when these breezy heights knew not the cheap tripper, when
> glass houses did not exist, when automatic machines were
> undreamt of. But that time has passed away for evermore,
> unless, indeed, a new generation shall arise that knows not the
> cockney, that insists on relegating such monstrosities to a
> humbler position, where they shall neither spoil the scenery
> nor cry aloud, 'Here I am! if you want meat or drink or
> packets of sweet stuff or sunbaked cigarettes—or penny surprise
> packets—or sham jewellery, come, oh come to me!' But will
> that time ever arrive? I trow not.

He trowed wrong. There are no toll fees today and the Torrs
belong to the National Trust. The glass restaurant at the summit
has long since been destroyed, and, in retrospect, those sunbaked
cigarettes and penny surprise packets seem delightfully innocent. But more was destroyed than the glass restaurant—fine
Victoriana that gave the town its character, like the authentic
wrought-iron bandstand on the front, which was sold for scrap
after the last war. A small thing perhaps, but an indication that
Ilfracombe did not care much for its heritage.

With such disregard, the destruction of the Ilfracombe Hotel
was inevitable. It was never the loveliest of buildings, but this
great Victorian edifice had style and suited the crenellated character of the town. The rot set in literally when the Army Pay
Corps was billeted there in the last war and, allegedly, stripped
lead off the roof. Even so, the Holiday Inn, as the hotel had

become, was sufficiently intact to be used for entertainment and council offices and sufficiently attractive for a Dutch businessman to offer a reputed million pounds to take it over. This was opposed by local interests and finally, though narrowly, rejected by the council.

In 1974 the North Devon County Council (now responsible for Ilfracombe) declared the building unsafe and asked for permission to demolish it. This was opposed by a large section of the town, 16,583 people signing a petition of protest. The Ilfracombe Architectural and Preservation Society accused the council of acting with 'undue secrecy and indecent haste, without the people of Ilfracombe being allowed to voice their opinion fully', and they suggested it was hardly a coincidence that the council evacuated the building on the eve of their request to the Secretary of State for a listing. Also, they laid the serious charge that the council was deliberately allowing the building to fall into disrepair, even ripping up floorboards for fences so that it would become unsafe.

A turbulent three-day public enquiry was held in January 1976 but those inexorable wheels had been set in motion and the council received their permission to destroy in July. The demolition was completed by March 1977.

It could be worse. At least the council has no intention, as yet, of building another complex in its place. Bitter experience, and our eyes, confirm this would not be for the better. Whenever an old building is torn down the new is more tawdry. Threats to tear down the Pannier Market in Barnstaple have been resisted by the farmers' wives, fortunately as tough as their free-range chickens, but it is shocking that such destruction is even contemplated. Even when something important is conceived from scratch, like the £800,000 North Devon Leisure Centre in Barnstaple, the result is squat and uninspiring. It is beside the river yet no advantage has been taken of the position, suggesting that the architect has not even visited the site; though of course he must have done. The prize attraction was an indoor swimming pool that proved to be short of Olympic standards by a matter of inches—I wonder who paid for the alterations. The bleak exterior would hardly matter if this were a factory, but it is disappointing when leisure and entertainment are concerned.

Though there are reports of a £450,000 development scheme for the Victoria Pavilion, the Holiday Inn will give way to open space and a view of Wildersmouth Bay that has been hidden for the last hundred years. If the council is brave enough there could be a semi-tropical garden to bear comparison with Tresco in the Scillies. It might be magnificent. The climate is surprisingly mild in winter and though an exceptional frost could cause casualties it is worth the risk. It will take time, but Tresco was a barren, windswept island when Augustus Smith bought the lease in 1834 and started his planting with species brought to him from all over the world. When he died in 1872 the full glory was yet to come, but he had the satisfaction of knowing that the Abbey Gardens would be a continuing, *living* delight for each succeeding generation. The same could happen here. The gardens that exist to the side, lit up at night in garish colours, are an attraction already. To make them spectacular will cost money, especially with a glass orangery for the rarest plants and a place to shelter in during rain, but it will be a fraction of the expense of a concrete complex.

It will need imagination—but that is what has been needed all the time. Think what might have happened after the war if Ilfracombe had exploited the Victoriana instead of tearing it down, reviving the town as *the* great Victorian resort. Then the Ilfracombe Hotel could have been restored easily to be the showpiece, and the High Street closed to all but horse-drawn traffic. This was a time when Victorian design had yet to be appreciated and was being smashed up all over the country. Priceless examples could have been saved as they have been for the Victorian street that is being constructed for the tramway museum at Crich— pillar-boxes, street-lamps and shop-fronts. A true music-hall could have provided genuine entertainment instead of the usual arch imitation, with a splendid Victorian pub to drink in. Old customs could be revived—'Donkey Chairs' to take children up the hill; Welsh women bringing cockles from Swansea on the morning steamer as they used to do; strings of coloured light-bulbs could decorate the harbour at night, with dancing in the open air at the site now used for the bus depot. A band in the bandstand, a bathing-machine on the beach. If presented with flair and fun, people would have flocked from all over the world.

A flight of fantasy? Of course, but something like that was needed and, ironically, the cost would have been minimal, for the assets of Ilfracombe would have been exploited instead of torn down and replaced. As it is, it cannot even be said that Ilfracombe has come to the end of the line. The line was closed in 1970.

When I came here first to see my parents, it was possible to take a train straight through from Waterloo to Ilfracombe in six hours. Today you have to change at Exeter, take the train to Barnstaple, and walk across the bridge to wait at the bus-stop unless you wish to take a taxi. The day-tripper has been replaced by the coach tourist and the independent visitor is rare. As the coaches take a large share of the profits away, the change has not been lucrative. This is one of the troubles in making grandiose plans for the future—Ilfracombe is poor.

When John Fowler organised his competition to name the coast, someone suggested 'Costa Geriatrica'. It was painfully apt. Ilfracombe has become the haven for couples who spent happy holidays here and think of buying a house on their retirement. An estate agent whisks them up the hill and flings open the window on to a glorious view—every house has a glorious view. When they return for good they are whisked up the hill again by a taxi. Soon they discover that if they manage to walk down the hill they have a hell of a climb back. When one partner dies, the other is left virtually a prisoner in their own home. It is tough to be old in Ilfracombe. Out of the population, a little over eight thousand, it is 'presumed' that 30 per cent are over retirement age—double the national average. As 15 per cent of the population are unemployed it means that almost half the town is supporting the other half. This is an unworkable balance already and the retirement age group is still pouring in, unaware that Ilfracombe is not the Mecca they remember—paradise out of season. If not discouraged, at least they should be informed of what to expect. Many are unable to afford the small luxuries so vital when you are old and live on your own: one welfare worker discovered an old lady who had not eaten a hot meal in three years. In our topsy-turvy society they are the first to suffer.

While Sidmouth and Exmouth attract retired people with money, Ilfracombe is for those on fixed incomes: 'If you want to send a bank manager to an early grave, send him to Ilfracombe!'

Some people believe it will need a massive introduction of light industry to prevent Ilfracombe deteriorating beyond recall. I wonder; there is something so fiercely independent about Ilfracombe that I hope for the best. There is a stronger sense of community than exists in Barnstaple: the old have a stoicism that rises above the material.

And the town is still delightful. I feel pleased whenever I enter it: no new towers have marred it yet, as they have the other resorts; you can stumble by happy accident on splendid corners like Adelaide Terrace, which convey all the grandeur of the great Victorian past though a coat of paint would be welcome. Much has been torn down, little has been put up, but the original character has not been lost altogether.

The Campbell Steamers still arrive from the Welsh coast; a Tourist Information Centre has just been opened at a cost of £14,000; there is even an Edwardian Bar—the revival could take place, though it is a vicious circle with no money to boost a new prosperity. It is a state of mind as much as economics. In the tradition of the Scottish landlady who locked out a married couple because they returned after midnight—'It's not decent!'—Ilfracombe is surprisingly prim with all its snobbish talk of Blackpool. There were so many complaints about the noise from Alexandra's Night Spot, where artists had to work to a decibel machine, that the management abandoned it at the end of 1976. Now the Council have taken it over: one can only hope they will be ambitious artistically if not economically. It is not an expensive face-lift that is needed, but a change of heart. Whenever I walk down to the harbour or along the tree-lined quay at Bideford, I imagine what it would be like with tables and chairs outside offering simple food and drink, with coloured lights and music in the evening. The food need not be fancy—and if a live group is not available, as it is in every pleasure garden in the smallest town in Romania, taped bazouki could be played. On my one visit to Watchet, further up the coast, there was dancing in the main square on a Saturday night and it seemed to be enjoyed by everyone, enhancing the entire atmosphere.

One of the most attractive features of a Mediterranean coastal town is the promenade in the evening when the road is closed to traffic and the people wander up and down the harbour front as the sun sets—and this costs nothing.

But the end of the pier at Ilfracombe is used as a car park. I recognise similar thoughts from Mrs Wilson, who has travelled round the world, lived with her husband in Canada, and recently went on holiday to Russia, but has never lost her particular love for Ilfracombe:

> Hillsborough is one of the few places in England from which the sun can be seen as it rises and sets in the sea, and our natural harbour is unusual as there are not many on the north coast of Devon and Cornwall. I adore all our beauty spots. Many people when looking at Ilfracombe from Hillsborough think the town has a very continental look. I wish the houses, shops and hotels would paint or colourwash their walls, like they do abroad, it would make it look so bright and cheerful, against the blue of sea and sky.

Am I one of those who believe standards have deteriorated? I am afraid so. Of course every generation complains that things are not the same—they never have been—but there is a point when you only have to look around you to know it is true. If a perfect stretch of coastline is overdeveloped, with shoddy buildings that need to be repaired before they are even completed, it must deteriorate. If you pull down an old farmhouse with a thatched roof and replace it with a horizontal concrete matchbox, the change must be for the worse. Would they improve Venice if they 'developed' it? I ask you! It is not just the buildings, nor the services like the post, which was delivered three times a day in Ilfracombe and once on Sundays, nor the trains that ran, but the sense of fun and thoughtfulness that prompted passengers on the old Barnstaple to Lynton railway to scatter packets of flower seeds from the windows to brighten the banks on the side of the narrow gauge track where the old steam train puffed across the countryside. Would people take such trouble now, or would they regard it as foolish?

It is hardly constructive to lament the past unless to signpost the future, so I offer these ideas:

Preserve the unspoilt by exploiting the resorts, like Ilfracombe and Westward Ho!, the perfect holiday centres. Newquay treats tourism like the industry it is and acts as the invaluable shock-absorber to such villages as Port Isaac and Port Gaverne.

Car parks should not be dumped on the front or in the centre of town but placed sensibly above, as they are in St Ives, so that the visitor has to walk down, which is a pleasure in itself. Never allow a car park against the skyline. In Polperro, where they have made it too easy, tourism has invaded the village which is overrun with pixies and people.

Coaches should not be allowed *into* any coastal village.

Lanes should not be widened, for this will encourage the flow of traffic.

Ban new buildings within a mile of the coast, apart from resorts.

Tree planting should begin on a large scale to help further preservation and conceal some of the monstrosities already up.

Naturalists, bird-watchers, walkers should be especially encouraged to come to the district for they appreciate it.

The Taw and Torridge Estuary should be declared a bird sanctuary.

Do not be deceived by the long hot summer of '76, but make allowance for both visitors and residents in Ilfracombe if it rains.

I am uncertain what is planned for the Victoria Pavilion, but the planners should think big, in terms of a modern Pleasure Garden celebrating the arts and music, food and drink, boats and ice-skating, and special summer shows—like the Tivoli Gardens in Copenhagen.

Build a conference centre in Ilfracombe, where the Holiday Inn would have been ideal. Envisage American conferences arriving at Chivenor by jumbo jet, instead of going invariably to London or Edinburgh. They will have the whole of the West Country within driving distance.

With every plan, consider its effect in fifty years' time.

This is Britain's favourite holiday area, attracting 23 per cent of 'home holiday travellers' which equals the South, Wales and Scotland put together. Ten million visitors bring £300,000,000, but at the moment the publicity boast that Ilfracombe is 'the door and dormitory to the West' is an empty one. Every effort should be made to restore Ilfracombe as a great resort, and this in turn will protect the local villages from being overrun instead.

Meanwhile, I salute the sixteen thousand who cared enough to sign the petition protesting against the abolition of the old Ilfracombe Hotel. Right or wrong, good luck to all difficult people who refuse to be mollified by the assurances of officialdom.

chapter fourteen

The villages of Ham and Appledore

Hereupon I dismissed the boys, who, with several rounds of
cheers, had escorted me through Braunton; and with genuine
thankfulness I gazed at the quiet and pleasing prospect. So
charming now in the fall of the leaf, what would it be in the
spring-time, with the meadows all breaking anew into green,
and the trees all ready for their leaves again? Also these bright
red Devonshire cows, all belonging to Polly, and even now
streaming milkily—a firkin apiece was the least to expect of
them, in the merry May month. A very real feeling of deep
peace, and the pleasure of small things fell on me . . .

from *Maid of Sker* by R. D. Blackmore,
set in North Devon in 1794.

Another reason for living here is the courtesy of village life. I am
lucky that Georgeham is within walking distance; it's known
locally as Ham, which means homestead, settlement or water-
meadow. It surrounds the Norman church of St George, which
was referred to in 1231, when Robert de Edington was 'persona

de Hamme', and in 1635 when the village was called Ham St George.

Down a slope with a farm to the right and Stevenson Balfour's Crowberry Cottage to the left, and you come to a group of thatched houses with a cottage at the end beside the stream where Henry Williamson conceived *Tarka*. Then the churchyard, higher up the stream, where my father and mother are buried below the fourteenth century tower. S. H. Burton describes it in *The North Devon Coast* as 'the prettiest and most poetical that a man could hope to see—or to rest in'.

The inscription on my father's tomb is simple: 'Negley Farson—Writer—Born Plainfield U.S.A. 1890—Died Vention 1960—He lived 18 years in this Parish.'

Other inscriptions are more colourful: one to the memory of William Kidman of the HMS *Weazel*, wrecked off Baggy Point in 1799; another to Simon and Julia Gould who lived together for seventy-four years and died at the age of a hundred, though their tombstone has been removed; and a mournful verse for Philip Gosse:

> In pain and sickness long I laid,
> My speech was stopt, my lungs decayed,
> I like a flower once did bloom
> But now lie mouldered in this tomb.

Another verse, more robust, honours the memory of Sergeant John Hill of the 40th Regiment of Infantry—'Waterloo man and through the Peninsula War with the Duke of Wellington: Died 28 February 1861, aged 77':

> Nor cannon roar, nor rifle shot
> Can wake him in this peaceful spot;
> With faith in Christ and trust in God
> The sergeant sleeps beneath this clod.

The most poignant is the epitaph to a father by his son:

> Reader who are thou that passeth by
> And on this place moulds chance to cast an eye.
> Here lies a man beneath this stone

As worthy as this world has known
His labour hands provid his daily bread
His pious care his children taught and fed
His ready honesty full kept its ground
Unshaken whither fortune smils or frown
His well spent life all dread of death supress
And smooth his passage to Eternal rest
So may his son with modesty may say
That this to his father's memory pay.

As Stevenson Balfour comments in his history of *Georgeham and Croyde*, 'Even allowing for filial love, what man can expect more.'

It is a pity that Mr Balfour's 'history' is out of print for it is full of information, such as the background to the most mysterious epitaph of all:

In loving remembrance of P.C. Walter Creech
who died in the execution of his duty
July 29th 1883, aged 31 years.

Apparently it was a Saturday evening at seven o'clock when a local character, referred to by Mr Balfour as 'Mr G', was drinking at the King's Arms opposite the church. After several glasses of beer he made so much noise that P.C. Creech came in and told him to be quiet as he could be heard all over the village.

With the bonhomie of drink, Mr G asked the policeman to join him but received the blunt reply, 'Not from the likes of you,' which was highly provocative to someone already inflamed. Mr G became abusive and was taken home by a Mr Bale, a friend from Barnstaple, muttering that he had a knife and would kill the——. Far from passing out, Mr G left his house shortly afterwards and was seen talking to a villager. P.C. Creech, who was obviously on the prowl, then made the fatal mistake of interrupting them, putting his hand on Mr G's shoulder as he urged him to go back home again.

'Mr G made a feint at the constable with a stick and drew a knife from his pocket, thrusting it into the policeman's left side.' The doctor was fetched at a quarter to six the next morning from Braunton, but P.C. Creech was dead when he arrived. The post mortem showed that the knife had cut a piece off a rib and penetrated the stomach.

Meanwhile, Mr G had been wandering around Georgeham, threatening other villagers with his knife, until he staggered back to his home. A small crowd collected outside as P.C. Rich from Braunton, helped by Mr Bale, shouted to Mr G to come out. Some people remarked that P.C. Rich was a coward, and Mr Bale told him to ignore them. Anyhow it was Mr Bale who leapt on his friend when he came out, caught him by the collar, and forced him over the wall until he was handcuffed.

The inquest took place on Monday, appropriately at the King's Arms, in front of the Chief Constable of Devon. A verdict of wilful murder was returned and Mr G was taken by dog-cart to Braunton and then by train to Barnstaple where he was put in the lock-up. His case came before Baron Huddlestone on 8 November 1883, but the prison surgeon reported that Mr G was too ill to stand trial and, sure enough, he died that afternoon.

There were mitigating circumstances, as they say. Mr G was usually a contented man who kept bees and made his living by selling their honey. Once he brought a charge against some boys who had thrown stones at the bees; it was dismissed. This could explain his dislike of the police who had already summonsed him for drunkenness. After this he had remained teetotal for two years, but he had started again with renewed violence in 'his cups'. A trace of Mr G remains with the beehives set in the wall near the village shop where he used to have his cottage. And there is a poignant postscript underneath the epitaph to P.C. Creech, revealing that a son was born shortly after his death but died in infancy nine months later.

The King's Arms is still flourishing, run by Mr and Mrs Olliver, the most tolerant of landlords considering that they are teetotal. Now it has been renovated and is crowded out in summer. R. W. Thompson recalls quieter times in *Home in Ham*, such as the arrival of electricity one evening in 1937:

It was about a week later that light suddenly flared in the bar parlour of the King's Arms. We blinked our eyes at it. Charlie and his 'Missis' stood looking somewhat sheepish, somewhat proud, somewhat defiant, behind the bar. Stanley was in the corner-seat hard up against a roaring fire that scorched his trousers, and gave us an expectancy of the pungent odour of roasting flesh. Percy, in his corner opposite, hung his head, seeming bewildered, seeking the shadows in which he had been wont to rest since HM Royal Navy had said he had done enough.

Old Brownie sat upright under the shuttered window that throws the shapes of two hearts against the stone wall across the way. Old Brownie removed a stub of clay pipe from amongst his whiskers and dipped his walrus moustache in his pint, and didn't care much about lights so long as the flavour he knew so well was in the beer.

'That's all right, m'dear,' he droned in his rasping groan of a voice. 'Tha's all right. Don't worry, m'dear!'

Alec hovered around the skittle-board, eyes darting from one to the other of us, back and forth.

'Well, us can see ter play now,' he said with a quick grin. And as he spoke we all knew that we were making excuses in our minds for these 'ere lights. Charlie said: 'Well, I had it put. Makes a deal of difference.'

In the winter the King's Arms becomes a village pub again, reflecting village life, and the Ollivers go to endless trouble to create a happy atmosphere at Christmas with trays of food passed round by their daughter, music, and boisterous renditions by Bill Brown.

Surprisingly, there used to be four pubs in Georgeham. The Ring o' Bells is now Westend Farm, and at the Victoria Inn next to the churchyard, also known as the Church House, they brewed ale for the Rectory to help pay for the church expenses. Built in 1678, it is known as Millie's Cottage now, owned by John Boulton who runs a small china shop on the side, round the corner. Sharing his interest in the occult, his knowledge, conversation, and friendship have enhanced life considerably. The Rock Inn, further up the hill, has been taken over recently by Jim Ashford and has come to life again. The old pub has been extended but has been kept in a fine traditional style under the direction of Lesley Ashford, proving that it is possible to rebuild and actually improve. With her excellent home-cooked meals, the Rock has become a new meeting place for the village.

Will Georgeham be allowed to remain so perfect? Even in 1938, R. W. Thompson had his doubts:

> Ham was changing fast, not the essential Ham, but the overlay. Where there had been two strangers in the lanes and on the beaches, now there were a score. Ham was discovered. The writing is on the wall, and even rearing its ugly head above the high banks of the narrow Devon lane that leads down to Putsboro'—'Attractive building sites for sale'—it says. Soon they are going to begin 'improving Ham', but maybe a core that is real will remain.

It has, until now. The worst threat has come from a field on the side of the road to Braunton that was offered for a modest price by the late Porter Thomas to the local council, who considered using it as a car park to ease the congestion in the summer. This idea was opposed vigorously by a minority, and rejected. The trouble is, with a field on the market, that the alternative may be worse. Sure enough it was bought for a more handsome price by a builder who received planning permission from the Barnstaple Rural District Council in 1973 to build ten houses to the acre.

This is where the usefulness of 'difficult people' comes in. The Croyde Area Residents' Association, under the chairmanship of Tom Bigge, asked Jeremy Thorpe to call on the Minister of the Environment to intervene, especially as the villages of Georgeham and Croyde had just been designated as Conservation Areas. Yet, incredibly, or not so incredibly as far as government is concerned, the Minister 'appreciated' the objection and 'recognised' the special care that should be taken, but 'did not think his Department would be justified in intervening in this case, which he regarded as essentially one of local importance'. Mr Bigge made the restrained comment: 'I find this statement, to say the least, surprising. The protection of an Area of Outstanding Natural Beauty is surely not just of local importance. Coastal Preservation Orders are not merely of local importance. Steps are therefore being taken to bring the matter to the Minister again.'

Since then the figure of a hundred new houses has been disputed and when the application came before the Planning Committee it was rejected 'on the grounds that scale, density and design were considered to be unacceptable in view of the close proximity to a Conservation Area and the likely highway danger envisaged'. But the builders own that land meanwhile and anything could happen in the future.

There are many points of view but if you look at Georgeham today and envisage it in fifty years' time, surely there is only one conclusion.

There is no need for more houses; with no jobs waiting for people at Georgeham, they could be placed just as successfully somewhere else where the damage would be less traumatic. Georgeham may not be unique (though I believe it is), but the village is certainly a rarity.

As Braunton used to be.

Probably the saddest change in village life is the erosion from outside, the way that houses are bought by people who can afford to keep them as 'holiday homes' and leave them idle for most of the year. Admittedly I am a foreigner too, but this is my sole and permanent home. Not that the outsiders stand aloof, far from it: frequently they hurl themselves into the small community with all the brightness of the ad-man, organising local events at a pace that is neither suited to nor wanted by the village.

More seriously, they push up the prices and deprive young local couples of the chance to buy cottages that should rightfully be theirs, and this corrodes the heart of a community that was self-contained.

A village like Braunton could have withstood a siege a hundred years ago. When people complained of the noise they referred to the hammering of carpenters or the rattling of wheelbarrows. The din could be so excruciating that if someone was ill inside they laid straw over the cobbles to dull the clatter of the carts.

In *Victorian Days in a Devon Village*, A. H. Slee mentions eight carpenters, four blacksmiths and five shoemakers, and the communal life centred round the Cross Tree in the middle of the village, much as it does in France or Greece today. A local band played there on summer evenings; the winner of an 'apple dumpling competition' consumed sixteen in record time: and more entertainment was provided by a German band, an Italian accordionist, six bearded Russians with four performing bears, and street-singers with the latest ballads, like musical news-bulletins, relating such subjects as Jack the Ripper. You could buy the words afterwards for a penny.

Food was brought on handcarts: fishermen with fresh mackerel and herring; black cherries, and whortleberries from Exmoor; and 'Johnny Frenchie', a boy from Brittany who arrived with strings of onions.

Touring theatrical companies stayed for a week, giving a different performance every evening, and nigger minstrels came from Barnstaple. The great event for children was the Bostock and Wombwell Circus and Menagerie, which pitched their tents in a field that is now the Recreation Centre.

> We were in another world. [says Mr Slee] Elephants, bears, camels, lions, tigers and apes of every description were all wonders to boys whose only idea of a wild animal was a fox or badger, occasionally seen around the countryside, or a monkey perched on an Italian barrel organ. The performances with wild animals were thrilling and often frightening, especially when the roars of the snarling and growling lions seemed to rock the cages. I shall always remember the half-naked Zulus standing on a platform and throwing their assegais at a wooden target and never missing their aim. There were also a tattooed man and a bearded lady.

In those days the pubs, and there were four of them around the tree, were open from eight in the morning until ten at night and enjoyed a thriving business in spite of the risk of drunkards being denounced by the Town Crier in solemn but ringing tones: 'Last night in a certain house not far from here, a certain gentleman was brought home in a drunken condition . . .'

Now Braunton is several times the size—it claims the title of 'the largest village in England'—and the flavour seems to have gone. Individual crafts have proved too arduous or been driven out of business by the restrictions that discourage incentive today. Even the simplest occupations have become more complicated. Where a single man swept the open gutters on the side of roads with a brush and cart, it needs a lorry-load now with an official coming out from Barnstaple in his best clothes to inspect the work, and after all that the drains are blocked more easily than ever.

Communal life is dispersed: A. H. Slee, who knew Braunton better than most, comes to this sad conclusion: 'As the years have gone by houses have been modernised, and the cob and thatched houses are few and far between. Even the old Cross Tree, which had marked the site of the East Cross for many centuries, had to succumb to modern development schemes. The picturesque village of the '80s has now become a small suburban town with modern amenities.'

As for the holiday homes occupied, or rather *not* occupied by their new owners from outside, they do not affect Braunton, which oozes outwards. They have disturbed the pattern of simple fishing ports to the south like Brixham, and the change can be seen in Appledore on the other side of the Taw and Torridge Estuary. Already a sprawl of development called the Riversemeet Estate rises above the village, half against the skyline, while simple cottages are sold in old Appledore for sums that are far from simple. I can understand why people are so eager to pay for them, for Appledore contains attractive Georgian houses, with large windows on the upper floor to light the lofts used for sail-making. John Beara comments on this in his booklet *Appledore: Handmaid of the Sea*:

> In area the new Appledore is almost twice that of the old, but there has been no proportionate increase in population. The clue to this is partly to be found in the large number of holiday homes that are scattered throughout the narrow streets and lanes of the old town, most of them unoccupied for the greater part of the year, and in the considerable number of cottages at present empty for one reason or another.

Even so, Appledore is my favourite village in Britain. Mr Beara's booklet has a splendid centre-spread photograph of the quayside taken in 1890 it was rebuilt in 1938—and this picture proves that it must have been incomparable. In spite of all the changes and the tarmac that has replaced the cobbles, the zest is still there.

Appledore lives by the sea and for the sea, the backs of the houses tumbling into the water. The churchyard is filled with the graves of those who have given their lives to the sea, captains and pilots and master mariners like Thomas Smith of the schooner *Hazard*, who was drowned on a voyage from Lanelthie to Appledore and whose remains are interred at Larn—'October 31st 1859, aged 50 years'. Underneath there is the name of the son who drowned with him: Philip Green Smith, aged fifteen.

Appledore's entire existence has depended on the sea since the days of the Armada, when Queen Elizabeth declared the village a free port with the privilege of exemption from mooring dues. Writing in the seventeenth century, Thomas Westcote remembered the place when there were only two poor houses, but remarked that it had grown so 'for fair buildings and multiplicity of inhabitants and houses, it doth equal divers market towns, and is furnished with many good and skilful mariners'.

This skill has fostered Appledore through the years as a centre of shipbuilding for wooden sailing vessels, but a decline set in with the disappearance of sail. A slump began in the 1920s and nothing of any size was launched for the next twenty years. Shipbuilding came to a standstill and was only revived by the demands of war. In 1963, when the firm of P. K. Harris was forced into liquidation and their yards closed overnight, a new decline and unemployment seemed inevitable until Appledore was saved by the formation of Appledore Shipbuilders Ltd., which became one of the most successful examples of post-war private enterprise under the direction of Jim Venus. While he built the largest covered shipyard of its kind in Europe, launching a bulk carrier of 5,000 tons into the Torridge, another shipyard, J. Hinks & Sons, became famous for replicas of the Hudson Bay's *Nonsuch* and Drake's *Golden Hind*, authentic in every detail and now on exhibition at San Francisco.

This was a glorious revival, but in 1974 the Appledore Shipyards were nationalised and one can only fear for their future and hope that local initiative will triumph. Recent orders in 1976 indicate that it will.

Appledore is too down-to-earth, or down-to-sea, to be a tourist attraction like Clovelly. With Westward Ho! as the invaluable buffer nearby, it is isolated, on the way to nowhere, though I was startled to learn that the railway came here from 1908–17 with three steam engines, The Grenville, Torridge and Kingsley, struggling against the wind in winter as they tried to pull their carriages to Westward Ho! and Bideford.

The alleys behind the quay are too narrow for cars, which should be banned, and it is a village to explore on foot, discovering old cottages decorated with small figureheads or plates above the doorways; and the peeling façade of the former Gaiety Cinema with a mermaid announcing 'Continuous Performances'. On the shore opposite, where the old lighthouse used to stand, the salmon fishermen pull their nets, and ships outside wait patiently to ride the Bideford Bar when the tide is full, on their way to Bideford and Barnstaple.

Revels—regattas—and harvest homes

Held at the end of April, the Georgeham Revels were a popular village occasion until the motor-car interfered. Trestle tables laden with food were set up on the cobbles beside the church wall, and villagers danced to the music of the violin in the barn next to Crowberry Cottage.

The motor-boat has yet to interrupt the Appledore Regatta, though there is not the fierce competition of the old days when boats were built secretly in back yards and carried down to the water on Regatta Day to take their rivals by surprise and win the coveted prizes. But there is still the sense of occasion: visitors join the old men who are always leaning over the wall opposite the Seagate looking out to sea; a flash of boats cutting the water like blades, sometimes racing as far as Lundy Island; and old-fashioned sports like the greasy pole. It is wonderfully good natured with none of the candy floss, neon-lit seediness that has seeped into so many fairs today.

The regatta cannot have changed all that much. Towards the end of summer I witnessed another slice of English life that I thought had gone forever. This was the Harvest Home at East Brent, a peaceful patch of Somerset, where the villagers join together on the last Thursday in August to give thanks for the harvest—literally a 'thanksgiving'. Harvest Homes take place in various parts of the country but this is one of the oldest, started in 1857 by Archdeacon Denison and his 'near and dear friend' Mr Higgs the churchwarden. Apart from the religious ceremony, it was founded as a feast for the whole village, paid for by the far-

mers and wealthier members of the parish. In the early days the
sexes were segregated: the men and boys had lunch, the women-
folk in new dresses sat down for tea. There were steam engines
then, bringing steam-roundabouts and steam swing-boats and a
Punch and Judy Show. In the evening there were dances like the
lancers and quadrille, where everyone joined in. Popular from
the outset, it has been held for 119 years apart from a four-year
gap in the last war.

There is a feeling of expectancy from the moment the man
climbs Brent Knoll, which is 450 feet high overlooking the
church and the vicarage, and hoists a vast union jack that came
from a battleship, to the top of the flagpole. The church bells ring
out, echoing across the countryside, and shortly before eleven
there is the distant sound of music drawing closer as the Silver
Band from Burtle joins the procession that has been forming,
and the clergy go down to the village to lead them. First a choris-
ter carrying a banner, followed by the school children as the
band renders 'Onward Christian Soldiers' with Brownies,
invited guests including the local MP, ex-servicemen, the choir
headed by another banner, clergy, committees, parishioners and
visitors trailing behind.

When they reach the church they file inside with that slightly
self-conscious walk that English people adopt when they enter
museums or places of worship.

Nowadays the villagers pay £1.50 for their lunch and this year
450 sat down in the grand marquee, consuming 200 lb. of ham,
100 of roast beef and 150 of boiled beef, washed down with 165
gallons of beer and 30 gallons of cider. All the tickets have been
sold, raising nearly £700, and the rest of the cost (just over
£1,000) is raised throughout the year with cheese and wine parties, whist and skittles.

There are no gimmicks, no plastic, no politics; the butter
arrives in mounds instead of being wrapped in little bits of silver
paper, the cider has been made locally. It is all genuine and such
a self-contained affair that I would feel an outsider if the welcome were not so friendly. For everyone in the village takes part:
all the young men and women who wait on the others are volunteers. No one takes it too seriously, and the marquee is decorated
with embroidered banners:

Somerset born, Somerset bred
Strong in the arm, weak in the head.
Pudding today, Pill tomorrow
Despise school and remain a Fool
There's nothing like water.

There is the sound of applause, deafening as the villagers push their plates away and clap their hands in unison, as the hard-working band marches into the tent yet again heading the great parade of the Christmas Puddings, the traditional ritual even in August. Once they were made in the vicarage in special boilers and passed through the window by a lady who used a secret recipe that she promised to reveal on her death bed. Sadly, she collapsed unexpectedly, taking her secret to the grave, but they say the puddings are as good as ever and sixty of them are held high on their plates as the ladies march round the marquee. The puddings weigh between two and three pounds each and after they have been distributed a sense of well-being seems to permeate the tent, not even dampened by the perennial speech by the local Member of Parliament who starts with a risqué story concerning a Scotsman and his kilt.

The band has gone only to return again: this time the procession consists of a Monster Loaf, six feet of freshly baked bread and The Giant Cheese which is carried by four men and weighs 120 lb., worthy of a district that boasts such names as Cheddar Gorge and the Mendip Hills not far away. The Rector removes his coat and cuts the first slice, casting it to the assembled waiters below the high trestle table, who scramble to catch it, for the winner will have good luck for the next twelve months.

There is a speech from the local bishop and someone falls asleep; yawns and a muttering of 'Hear, hear' when the next speaker promises to be brief; outside the smaller children are assembling for a fancy-dress competition while the older ones compete in egg-and-spoon and sack races. As it grows dark the traditional fair lights up; a tug of war between teams of giants takes place in the marquee where the lunch has ended; soon there will be entertainment and dancing. Then the East Brent Harvest Home will come to an end, but only for another year, for this is a piece of country life that continues unmolested by progress.

chapter fifteen

The high tides of September

Three wives sat up in the lighthouse tower,
And they trimmed the lamps as the sun went down;
They looked at the squall, and they looked at the shower,
And the night-rack came rolling up ragged and brown.
But men must work, and women must weep,
Though storms be sudden, and waters deep,
And the harbour bar be moaning.

Three corpses lay out on the shining sands
In the morning gleam as the tide went down,
And the women are weeping and wringing their hands
For those who will never come home to the town;
For men must work, and women must weep,
And the sooner it's over, the sooner to sleep;
And good-bye to the bar and its moaning.

> From *The Three Fishers* by Charles Kingsley,
> referring to the old Braunton lighthouse two
> miles up river from Bideford Bar.

I have received a letter from a lady in Australia who left here eight years ago and yearns for the wetness of North Devon. Someone sent her my introduction to the Croyde Guidebook: 'If I feel low I read it and remember England and its green fields again. It is such a dry place in Townsville and with luck it rains every nine months or so. I came out here with Ballroom teaching certificates, but the climate is much too hot for such activities.'

She should have seen Croyde this August! There came a time in the long hot summer of '76 when it seemed the heatwave would never end. As fields turned brown and reservoirs ran dry, I imagined the effect if we went without rain for five years instead of five months. Already our way of life was changing, with siestas in the afternoon, but a heatwave is as unbecoming to England as smog to the desert.

The first blobs fell on the burnt earth at the beginning of the August Bank holiday, and then it started to pour. Soon there was the crazy situation in North Devon of people queuing up with buckets at standpipes while the heavens collapsed around them. Polperro was devastated by floods. Poor lady in Townsville, little wonder she envies us the most delightfully eccentric climate in the world.

After the fox (though I still have my doubts about that mink), we replaced the chickens at once before we lost our nerve. I missed those golden omelettes but it was not long before the new hens started providing us again. Then one of them went broody and we bought a clutch of eggs locally to let her sit on them. Peter and Frances left for a few weeks with careful instructions that I should do nothing. The eggs are due to hatch on the day of their return.

At first I obey this advice scrupulously until I begin to think of the wretched bird, locked inside its coop. One morning I let it out before I release the others from the hen house and it gives a shattering squawk of joy and a wild fluttering of wings. Never have I seen an animal so relieved. After strutting around the run it returns to the coop to sit on the eggs again. Later in the day I come with a bowl of warm water to clean the chicken, which was filthy, and now it regards me as a nurse as I let it out each morning, still beady-eyed but grateful.

Jack Boucher along the lane told me I could let the hen out for hours if I wanted and the eggs would come to no harm. He gave me a tip as well, to put the eggs in a bowl of water and see if they floated and were fertile—counting the chickens before they are hatched. By the time I did this I had forgotten if the fertile eggs float or sink, and felt guiltily that I might have disturbed the whole process of hatching. And what exactly *is* blood temperature? My fears are realised when the broody rises with a squawk a few days later for her morning's liberty and I see an egg with a chick halfway out and dead, embedded in the shell. Have I killed them all by plunging them in water? I do not release the hen the next morning and think I hear a faint 'cheep'; when Peter and Frances return in the afternoon we lift off the lid and a fluffy yellow chick emerges from the straw followed by another. Altogether there are nine hatched from the clutch of twelve: I feel immensely proud.

Fascinating to watch the baby chicks and see how they respond, imitating the hen instantly, following her every squawk, dipping their beaks in the bowl of water and tilting them up as if they are sampling it like wine-tasters. Pale yellow balls of fluff at first that become white or honey-brown, growing visibly in the sun while the hen cleans herself with a dust-bath. The whole process absorbs me: the way the hen shunted two eggs to the back sensing they were addled; and the lice and ticks that provided food for the chicks as they were born. Now their filthy nesting box has been removed and they explore their new run excitedly. When they return to the warmth of the hen, their bright yellow heads peek out in tiers, reminding me of tarts with dyed hair looking hopefully from their windows in a black, back street tenement in Naples.

Bassey is used to the other hens now as they wander freely about the garden, but memories of Ermintrude are revived as she sees the yellow chicks and she peers at them salaciously through the wire netting.

A glut of mushrooms

It is a rich time of year. Following the endless summer, the rains have brought the mushrooms. We discovered them by accident as we picked blackberries, half-strangled by the burnt-out grass.

With further rain I expected they might be more plentiful—
and they were. At first there was the childish satisfaction of finding the occasional mushroom as I crossed the fields above the
Marine Drive, then clumps together, still more further on—
large horse mushrooms—then a stretch of hillside where I find a
slope that is scattered with them. Elation at the first fairy ring,
thirty or more mushrooms, fresh and firm in a perfect circle. The
bag fills up. More rings and the pleasure becomes a chore—one
fairy ring an enchantment, but twelve ridiculous. As the bag
overflows the fun is gone but at least there are quantities for the
deep-freeze and Frances makes a miraculous soup that tastes as
rich as if it had been made with quantities of cream but in fact
could not be simpler.

A day of little achievement but much satisfaction. The summer is
far behind, yet the glow of September is continuing into October.
After letting the hens and the chicks out and feeding them, I open
the door for the dogs below, who are greeted hysterically by
Bonzo and bound down to the beach as soon as they realise I am
heading there myself. Bassey sticks halfway down the slatted
steps and hangs on grimly as I hurry to help her, but she slips
through. Fortunately the sandbank is just below and she tumbles
down without hurting herself, but I must not chance it again.

The light is extraordinary. The early morning sun has hit the
top of Baggy Point, giving a golden touch to the greens and
browns, picking out the white surf round the rocks below the
folds of the cliffs.

The moon is more vivid in the blue sky above me than when it
is dark, while the rising sun is yet unseen. The sea is limitless, an
end of the world emptiness that might be eerie except for the
reassuring shape of Lundy Island on the horizon and the solitary
figure of a night-time fisherman further along the beach. A passing coaster heads for the Bristol Channel. I have never seen a
view so clean.

A high tide and the beach is strewn with seaweed and wood. I
find a small hand-woven basket that is old but perfectly intact
and I fill it with cuttle-fish for the hens, a black ball for Streaker,
who would be bound to lose it in her dash along the surf with
Bonzo, and two wooden wedges. Carrying a long plank under my

arm as I collect the papers at the end of the lane, I meet Jack Boucher, who asks laconically, 'Wrecking?' I learn some country lore when the conversation turns to baked rabbit covered with fat bacon, and the deterioration of dripping: 'Don't allow cows to mature these days—no, can't find good dripping now. In the First War mother gave us bread and lard, she had to with butter at five shillings a pound—some people only made that in a week then. The same with a pig, they used to let 'em reach twelve to fourteen score before they killed them and mother used the entrails, head and all in a hog's pudding, the real stuff, not like today—can't tell whether to put jam or mustard on it, can you? Half would go to pay for the pig, his keep, and the butcher, with a piece for the salter—the other half we ate. Mother would melt the fat down and keep it in an earthenware jar; it would last for years.'

'Why do they kill them too soon now?' I asked.

'Food's too dear and they don't grow so much themselves. The farmers used to grind their own barley and crush their own corn. Now it's all those pellets.'

'The easy way out?'

'Exactly!'

The end of the year

I am constantly aware of the seasons here.

In the spring I looked out from my balcony and the sea was so high and the waves so tempting that I ran down to the sands for the first swim of the year, though dip might be a more truthful description of it. I felt so refreshed mentally that it must have done me good physically, or vice versa. My batteries recharged, I could sympathise with the feelings of Charles Kingsley when he wrote of returning to Devon constantly to be 're-magnetised'.

Now the winter has returned like an angry man: a storm shakes the windows with such impatience that two panes have been broken, and the door of the dogs' outhouse was flung open at four in the morning forcing them to huddle in the porch.

The ground has hardened, and when I return along the beach after collecting the morning papers, Bonzo chases a seagull and skids on the ice that has formed on part of the sand. She picks herself up and steps away perplexed until her back legs slip in different directions so that she seems in serious danger of splitting. Like a skater, she recovers her balance in time.

It is glorious weather because it is so vigorous.

The morning post brings one of the rewards of living here: the first advance copy of my latest book. This is a satisfying moment, adding it to the shelf with the others, better than publication day or the first reviews. Today it is still strange and new. Tonight I may start reading it for the last time. I never understand when people say a writer's life is lonely: I find such kinship with the written page that the very look of words on paper is reassuring. Of course it is a mad profession these days, struggling against the tide of contracts delayed in the post, cheques that fail to arrive; and the dribble of one third of the advance on acceptance, one third on delivery and a third on publication.

It is hard to make a living as a freelance writer in England now, except for the brilliant few like John Le Carré, who wrote to encourage me before the publication of *Out of Step*: 'we do from the heart wish you luck and joy; sod the reviewers, don't give away too many free copies (we have ordered ours from Heywood Hill) and remember that the English *hate* their writers as only illiterates can'.

But for me there is no alternative.

The post also brings an incoherent letter from a man living somewhere illegible in Wales who has read my article in the *Spectator* 'In Defence of Dogs'.

> Daniel Farson—Those *awful*, bloody awful dogs . . . the whole lot should be rounded up and disposed of in a huge gas chamber. Your article is pure parody. If you were not blind or dishonest or both you would agree that 99 % of the dogs encountered outside police stations, farms etc., are ugly repulsive noisy lousy nuisances. In fact it would be virtually impossible to find any domestic dog that is not (a major or minor) nuisance to the owner's near neighbours or to someone somewhere. *This is the absolute indisputable undeniable truth about dogs.*

At least the man is definite.

I work until late in the afternoon, when I take my own dogs—

restless if not bloody awful—for a long walk. A tractor conspicuous on the skyline, is dropping hay for the cows that follow it eagerly, or try to; they are held back by two tense sheepdogs who leap at them aggressively, nipping their tails as they swing round. Looking back when I reach the top of the hill, I see the roof of my house, Baggy Point, and the raging white Atlantic; another storm is gathering; the view is an exhilaration in itself. The dogs raise the ancient hare that lives near Pickwell and go squealing in pursuit with Streaker in front and Pencil, despite her age, a hair's breadth behind. Now that the season is over and the car park closed, her fantasy life is suspended.

The tide is just a few feet away from the steps and the surf so wild that I decide to brave it, though it is November; this will be my last swim of the year. I am rewarded. The water is warmer than June and I come out glowing from the buffeting.

Dinner consists of mackerel caught earlier in the year and smoked, with Frances's home-made bread, two baked rabbits, snared, vegetables from the garden, and pears from the espaliered tree, baked in fresh elderberry juice instead of the usual red wine, and far better. I can hardly imagine a more luxurious meal.

There is the first log fire of autumn. Bassey catches my eye as I drink my tea afterwards. Contrary to all expectation, it has not been Bassey to die before Christmas, but her daughter Alice. A liver disease coupled with arthritis caused her to waste away. Though the vet assured me there was nothing I could do for her, I blame myself bitterly for not being there to hold her when she was put to sleep. She deserved that; I hope I shall not be so cowardly the next time.

As for the indomitable Bassey, I looked back on the dunes a few days ago to see her stumbling round in circles. Though she is extemely heavy now, Peter managed to carry her back home where she has fought for and made, a slight recovery. Although partially paralysed, she is as jaunty as ever, her head permanently tilted in an expression of surprise, as if she is at half mast. And outside she remains as alert as ever; if she scents a rabbit near the house she gives a drunken lurch and manages to run a few yards before she falls. Dogs may have no concept of age or death, but this gay old dog is a remarkable example of the stamina of mind over limb. There is no hair left on the end of her tail, but it thumps on the floor as contentedly as ever as she looks up lopsidedly in hopes of tea.

A gale is blowing by the time I go to bed and the Atlantic is rattling at my window. I open my new book but I am too tired to read it for long. Bonzo gives a yawn and forms herself into a circle at the foot of the bed. Bassey on blankets in the corner thumps her tail gently. I turn out the light and fall asleep quickly. The day has not been long enough. Nothing really happened, but you may understand why I exchanged the glittering prizes for the grey stone house by the sea.

> Strong and free, strong and free,
> The floodgates are open, away from the sea.
> Free and strong, free and strong,
> Cleansing my streams as I hurry along
> To the golden sands, and the leaping bar,
> And the taintless tide that awaits me afar,
> As I lose myself in the infinite main,
> Like a soul that has sinned and is pardoned again.

> from Kingsley's *The Water Babies*,
> (a verse based on the River Torridge).

Postscript

The comfortable closing lines of a chapter can prove as deceptive as one of the sunsets you see here, when a molten ball plunges into the sea beside Lundy Island, and the sky turns scarlet after a flash of green. Draw the curtains the next morning and the day is bleak.

Not that the outlook is grey for me, but it has changed. It must seem ironic after all I have written; but there comes a moment when it is necessary to shift anchor again. Soon I shall be moving, but only to a wilder spot along this same stretch of coast-line.

Another window is opening.

Daniel Farson
April 1977
Vention